PRAYER
IN THE BLACK TRADITION

PRAYER
IN THE
BLACK TRADITION

O. Richard Bowyer
Betty L. Hart
Charlotte A. Meade

THE UPPER ROOM
Nashville, Tennessee

Prayer in the Black Tradition

Copyright © 1986 by The Upper Room
All rights reserved.

No part of this book may be reproduced in any manner whatsoever without written permission of the publisher except in brief quotations embodied in critical articles or reviews. For information address The Upper Room, 1908 Grand Avenue, P.O. Box 189, Nashville, Tennessee 37202.

We are greatly indebted to the men and women who have given us permission to include their prayers in this collection. While we have earnestly sought to contact all authors and copyright holders of protected works, if we have failed in any case to do so, we will correct the citation in future editions of this book. Please see the Acknowledgements at the end of the book for a listing of registered copyrights.

Cover Design: Steve Laughbaum
Book Design: Thelma Whitworth
First Printing: June 1986 (7)
Library of Congress Catalog Card Number: 85-52019
ISBN: 0-8358-0538-7

Printed in the United States of America

In loving remembrance of our mothers, whose unspoken prayers have surrounded our lives with God's love and grace:

Mrs. Jean Athella Morris Bowyer
Mrs. Mary Ellen Craney Meade
Mrs. Ruth Elizabeth Moatz Powell

CONTENTS

Introduction 9
1. Prayer in the Black Tradition: An Overview ... 13
2. Prayer for Public Worship and
   Special Occasions 19
3. Prayer for Personal Devotions 61
4. Prayer in Black Literature 82
5. Prayer in Song 95
   Acknowledgments 110
   Index 111

INTRODUCTION

Black Christians have been a part of American Methodism from the beginning. In 1976 the United Methodist Church established a new missional priority: Developing and Strengthening the Ethnic Minority Local Church. One important result has been the discovery of the rich heritage in United Methodism provided by its ethnic members.

The inspiration for *Prayer in the Black Tradition* came from an awareness that there are very few resources which document this heritage or offer access to the richness of black spirituality. This resource is intended not only for black Christians, as a celebration of their prayer tradition, but also for all other Christians whose prayer life may be deepened as they understand and experience the vitality and passion of another tradition.

For ten years I served as pastor of a predominantly black congregation. As I sought to lead my congregation in worship, I was often conscious of a style and tradition of prayer which was a part of their heritage but not mine. I felt that it would enrich my life and the worship experience of the congregation if we had a resource on which to rely in fashioning our prayers. Also, many younger black clergy have grown up in predominantly white churches or attended predominantly white seminaries. I believed that this resource could strengthen them in their lives and ministry. Finally, I hoped that such a book might be a means of preserving a significant aspect of our mutual heritage.

I consulted with Ms. Charlotte Meade, choir director at Trinity United Methodist Church in Fairmont, West Virginia, and a member of the editorial committee that prepared *Songs of Zion*; we decided to pursue the project. We approached Mrs. Betty Hart, a member of Trinity and an Assistant Professor of English at Fairmont State College where she has taught black literature. After the idea was approved by the Administrative Council, a proposal was sent to the Funding Committee of the West Virginia Conference Ethnic Minority Local Church Task Force. The proposal was to produce a collection of prayers and comments on "Prayer in the Black Tradition" for use in the black churches of the conference. The Task Force thought it worthy of consideration by the General Board of Discipleship. From there the proposal was referred to The Upper Room.

Prayer in the Black Tradition is the culmination of months of work. We have taped and transcribed prayers at various meetings and services. We have received statements and prayers from many people. We have also reviewed literature and songs and various other devotional resources. What follows is the result of those efforts.

The book has been organized to give an introduction and overview of the role of prayer in the black tradition and to provide a collection of prayers and comments for use in both public and private worship.

Chapter one, "Prayer in the Black Tradition," puts into context the prayers which follow. It includes the reflections of former slaves and noteworthy black clergy and laity.

Chapter two provides prayers for public worship and special occasions. The prayers are organized in the following categories: Invocations and Pastoral Prayers; Prayers before the Sermon; Closing Prayers and Benedictions; Altar Prayers; and Prayers for Special Occasions.

Chapter three is intended for personal devotional use. Statements about the value of prayer are included as well as powerful personal prayers from various lay and clergy persons.

Chapters four and five explore prayer in literature and song. While there has been much written about the meaning and power of music in the black tradition, very little has been written about prayer. Black literature speaks much of religion, worship, and song. But the work of Betty Hart and Charlotte Meade in these sections makes a unique contribution to the preservation of the black heritage.

The conclusion by Charlotte Meade invites others to continue the work that has been begun in *Prayer in the Black Tradition*. The task is to keep alive the various traditions which make United Methodism a force for meaning and a source of joy for millions of Christians.

Thanks and appreciation are in order for all who have made this book possible. These include the members of Trinity Church and of the Ethnic Minority Local Church Task Force of the West Virginia Conference. Mrs. Georgiana J. Brooks, a member of Trinity, and an outstanding Christian educator in the former Washington Conference of the Central Jurisdiction, has provided numerous suggestions and helped us to acquire many of the contributions included. Typing and retyping of drafts and correspondence has been done by Roberta Austin and Ella Tate. The North Central (WV) Opportunities Industrialization Center has contributed typing time for us as well. The support and encouragement of my wife Faith is deeply appreciated.

Above all we are grateful for our own experience in the black church and tradition and the many ways that have strengthened and enabled us to worship, to work, to witness, and to pray.

O. RICHARD BOWYER

1

PRAYER IN THE BLACK TRADITION
AN OVERVIEW

O. Richard Bowyer

There are clear analogies between the experiences of black people and the Egyptian bondage of the ancient Hebrews. Indeed, there are parallels with all the sufferings and subsequent captivities of the Jews. Those peoples and persons who have experienced or are experiencing oppression, rejection, persecution, and discrimination can find a great source of strength and encouragement in the religion of black people.

Even so, there is a quality about the black experience that is unique. No other people have suffered in quite the same way, nor endured the same indignities.

According to Willard A. Williams, formerly Director of the United Methodist Multi-Ethnic Center at Drew University:

> Prayer in the Black Tradition is the very center of the Christian life of Black people and continues to be the basis of hope. In those days when they dwelt in the dark valley of bondage hope was yet unborn. It was through prayer in which they found solace and temporary escape from their sordid condition. Many gathered surreptitiously in the back woods under the shadow of darkness to commune with God in prayer. The prayers were so fervent, they

seemed to ring up heaven. A significant and cogent feature of the prayers was the theological and sociological aspects. Their God was the same God of Abraham, Isaac and Jacob; a captain who never lost a battle; a God of unrelenting love and forgiveness. Yet their prayers were always mindful of their brothers and sisters who shared some hope for freedom some day. Out of this tradition most of us were raised and conditioned. By precept and example prayer was uplifted as an anchor and a balm for a troubled breast:

> There is a balm in Gilead, to make the wounded whole,
> There is a balm in Gilead, to heal the sin sick soul.

Today in an unsupportive society, prayer for Black people is still the "soul's sincere desire."

Writing of *The Spirituals and the Blues*, James H. Cone says, "The black slaves' response to the experience of suffering corresponded closely to the biblical message and its emphasis that God is the ultimate answer to the question of faith.

In the spirituals, the black slaves' experience of suffering and despair defines for slaves the major issue in their view of the world. They do not really question the justice and goodness of God. It is taken for granted that God is righteous and will vindicate the poor and the weak. Indeed it is the point of departure for faith. The singers of spirituals, another concern, centered on the *faithfulness* of the community of believers in a world full of trouble. They wonder not whether God is just and right but whether the sadness and pain of the world will cause them to lose faith in the gospel of God. They are concerned about the solidarity of the community of sufferers. Will the wretched of the earth be able to experience the harsh realities of despair and loneliness and take this pain upon themselves and not lose faith in the faithfulness of God? There was no attempt to evade the reality of suffering.

Black slaves faced the reality of the world "ladened wid trouble, an' burden'd wid grief," but they believed that they could go to Jesus in secret and get relief. They appealed to Jesus not so much to remove the trouble (though that was included), but to keep them from "sinkin' down."

> Oh, Lord, Oh, My Lord!
> Oh, My Good Lord! Keep me from sinkin' down.
> Oh, Lord, Oh My Lord!
> Oh, My Good Lord! Keep me from sinkin' down.

Significantly, the note of despair is usually intertwined with confidence and joy that "trouble don't last always." To be sure, the slaves sing "Sometimes I feel like a motherless child, a long way from home"; but because they are confident that Jesus is with them and has not left them completely alone, they can still add (in the same song!), "Glory Hallelujah!" The same conjunction also occurs in:

> Nobody knows the trouble I've seen,
> Nobody knows my sorrow.
> Nobody knows the trouble I've seen,
> Glory, Hallelujah!

It may be helpful to look at the role of prayer in black worship in relationship to preaching and music. Writing in *Black Sacred Music and Social Change*, Wyatt Tee Walker notes:

Music is one of the three major support systems in Black Church worship. Preaching and praying are the other two. It is difficult to say conclusively which is the most important. . . .

Black preaching, traditionally, is more auditory than literary; that is, it is aimed primarily at the ear as the route to the heart as over against being aimed at the eye as the route to the mind. . . . Thus, the auditory character of Black preaching takes on a musical quality with many shades of pace and emphasis and very often with a pronounced intonation that is musical enough to have a "key." Could it be that the old-style preacher as well as the new-style preacher perceives that the rhythmic impact of music bears and shares in the message? It is well worth pondering. Consciously and/or unconsciously, the transfer is made to the preaching act. An almost identical analysis can be made of praying, the other chief support system in Black worship.

It has been both fascinating and perplexing to find so little written about prayer in the black tradition. This is especially so because of my own experience of prayer and its meaning and importance in the black church.

Perhaps one reason for the lack of resources on black prayer is the intensely personal nature of prayer as contrasted with music, preaching and other aspects of worship. Mrs. Thelma S. Dixon, in commenting on the meaning of prayer for her, remarks almost parenthetically, "I never like to say too much about my prayer life. I think about the Pharisee and the publican and I don't like to be compared."

It has been refreshing and exciting in conversation and correspondence to find our personal convictions confirmed. Prayer is meaningful. It is important. It is deeply associated with the black Christian tradition. One of my own most memorable experiences was in Liberia when, during the opening service of a revival, the black American preacher gave an altar call. People literally ran to the altar to pray and to have the minister pray for them.

In the American black church, the reaction is somewhat more subdued. But one can sense the same energy and power at prayer time. It is a time to open up. People are prepared to pray. I have been a pastor in both rural and urban white congregations. I have served in the very heart land of Appalachia where prayer is also important. I grew up in a family and a local church in which prayer was especially significant. Yet in no other context has prayer been so clearly a means of grace as in the black church.

Persons of all walks and stations of life are ready to pray. And they are likely to come to the mourners bench to kneel and pour out their problems and petitions to God. There is always a sense of freedom and relief. Burdens have been laid down. People leave the altar much as Matthew reported of the Wise Men who worshiped Jesus. They depart by another way.

Bishop Edward G. Carroll reflects on the role and meaning of prayer in the life of the black church.

> First of all prayer is conversation with God. It is a close identification with the source of our being. Sojourner Truth, it is said, always boasted about the fact that "Children, I've talked with God. I've talked with Him in the woods and in the fields." Prayer has meant a very great driving force, as well as survival, in our race. Let me say three things about prayer as it relates to the black people. It is conversation with God, being very close to God.
>
> First of all it's acknowledgement that this is God's world and that we are part of it. To the black man that was beaten down and persecuted and who almost lost his self-respect, (when you lose your self-respect you lose initiative), prayer was bringing dignity and self-respect to a person who was otherwise. As he talked with God he knew he wasn't a nigger, an ex-slave, he was a child of almighty God the Father. That was one thing.
>
> Second, I think very spontaneous prayer was an intense realization of what they were saying as they were saying it in talking with God. God was very close. He brought sustenance in the midst of famine. You know we've gone through many depressions. Black people are primarily poor people. They may not have possessed the material things of this world, but by their constant talk with God and being reinforced, probably backed up with sincere Bible reading, they knew that spiritual food was sufficient for their needs and would sustain them even though material food was short.
>
> Third, prayer sort of caught them up into what I call the

Kingdom. They were participants in the Kingdom. It was not, really it was not, pie in the sky or something after death. It was right here and now, expressed, of course, through the church. In this way prayer has been a very important part of the spiritual development of the black faith. It is a traditional part of the black experience.

When I was a pastor, the important services were the prayer meetings. They may not be in vogue now. We tried to meditate upon scripture and then give our witness and then pray fervently. Intercessory prayer was so important, praying for each other. There were risks, of course, in allowing prayer to be regarded as magic or manipulating the will of God or manipulating people. But I believe genuinely that it was submitting to the will of God and asking God for the best in the unfolding of one's personality and then, in that way, the victory.

Above all prayer to us, and I speak as a black person, was talking with God, not so much asking for this or that thing or even survival, but assuring God that we are on God's side. This is so important.

Prayer is a part of the richness and beauty of the black tradition. For those who have shared in it, the prayers and comments collected here will be a source of renewal and refreshment. Others may find this work a doorway into a religious experience that can enliven, encourage, and energize the soul.

O Lord, the God of Abraham, Isaac, and Jacob—God of our weary years, God of our silent tears, thou who hast brought us thus far on the way—lead us onward, enrich, enliven, encourage, engage, and empower us. May we come to know, whether for the first time, or anew, the richness and beauty, the glory and the strength of prayer in the black tradition. In the name of the One who came among us, shared and bore our burdens and griefs, and rolled our sins away like the stone in Gethsemane. Amen.

2

PRAYER FOR PUBLIC WORSHIP AND SPECIAL OCCASIONS

Church is very important in the black tradition and religious experience. To go to church, however, is not quite the same as for other people. Church carries an emotional dynamic. One needs to feel she or he is in church or has been to church.

The spirit, the dynamic of prayer, is important. How it is prayed is significant. One cannot really separate the method from the content. The language, the drawing on meaningful or relevant imagery, the recollection of other sources of strength and help are all valuable parts of the prayer life of black people.

Rev. Glenn A. Brooks observes that "prayer in the black tradition is made up of quotations from hymns, scripture, and sometimes clichés. It also rehearses the relationship between God and his creation. It is the ultimate drama where all of life is relived—sadness, despair, joy and hope."

In the prayers that follow, note the biblical imagery, the dependence on and reference to titles or phrases from well-known songs as well as specific references to the contemporary social order. As the slave quoted in *Lay My*

Burden Down said, "God is a momentary God." God is timely; therefore, effective prayer addresses God on a timely basis and in a timely way.

J. DeOtis Roberts vividly describes black worship in *Liberation and Reconciliation: A Black Theology*. He notes that all people

> need an experience of retreat. The Mount of Transfiguration is where we must seek refreshment, perspective, and empowerment. Worship, especially for the oppressed, must be such an exalted experience of spiritual renewal and empowerment. Black worship, composed of gospels, spirituals, sermons, and prayers must provide refreshment and renewal for travel-weary pilgrims in black skin. "Nobody Knows the Trouble I've Seen" and "Sometimes I Feel Like a Motherless Child" make immediate contact with the black experience. When such pieces are rendered in a white church, they are *art*, but in a black church, they are *worship*. When whites and blacks with a white outlook hear these songs, it is for them an *aesthetic* experience, but when those who are the black poor and those blacks who still remember their own past and who empathize with the present experience of the majority of blacks hear these songs, the Spirit descends—it is a *religious* experience. Tears drop from their eyes and some say "A-men." The more emotional shout or dance out of their sorrow-joy as the legacy of their bittersweet past unfolds to them as an *existential* experience. This is a vital part of the experience of forgiveness in the lives of blacks. The experience is so healing and "holing" that it sends the oppressed back into another week of unmerited suffering and enables them to endure it without losing their sanity. Surely a faith that can do this is worth having.

A further word about black worship may be helpful in understanding the style and content of prayer in the black experience. William B. McClain, writes in *Christianity and Crisis* (November 2 and 16, 1970):

Prayer for Public Worship and Special Occasions

Worship in the Black Church celebrates life. It celebrates the power to survive. It reflects a life-style of persons who live on the existential edge where the creative and the destructive, the wise and the foolish, the sacred and the secular, the agony and the ecstasy, the up and the down are the contrarieties of human existence in the presence of the divine. Life is affirmed with all of its complex and contradictory realities. As Lerone Bennett points out in *The Negro Mood*: "The Essence of the black tradition is the extraordinary tension between the poles of pain and joy, agony and ecstasy, good and bad, Sunday and Saturday." Such a tradition encourages responses of spontaneity and improvisation, and urges the worshiper to turn himself loose into the hands of the existential here and now where joy and travail mingle together as part of the reality of God's creation.

This is the soul of worship in the black tradition, the genius of the Black Church that cannot be created or approximated, not even by the avant-garde "happenings" and programmed spontaneity of the "hip" white churches. Such worship experiences reflect liturgy and theology arising out of the happenings of a people living on the cutting edge. It calls into question the sepulchers of the American white church and the inoffensive prudential morality that issues forth from theology more rationalistic than radical, from a liturgy that is more soothing than satisfying. Worship in the Black Church tradition is a creative experience, not a book slavishly followed or a ritual rehearsed.

Willard A. Williams observes that for the black tradition "the pastoral prayer carries as much importance as the sermon. Prayers have much more value when they are extemporaneous rather than read from a book of prayer."

Dr. M.L. Woodson speaks of the opening prayer in the worship service:

I believe that the opening prayer in church worship service is important and very much needed because its purpose is to establish communion with God at the very outset of the service. Generally, such prayers include expressions of thanksgiving for the many blessings bestowed upon us during the past week and gratitude for the protection of us from unforseen dangers and accidents which could have befallen so many. This prayer can be a hope and strength builder for so many persons who come to church on Sunday morning with this need. And for setting the record straight, this opening prayer can acknowledge our weaknesses before the Lord with our petition. Our forefathers used to say: "We come this morning like an empty pitcher before a full fountain, ready to be filled."

The prayers that follow come from a rich oral tradition and seem to cry out to be shared.

INVOCATIONS AND PASTORAL PRAYERS

Now, May the God Almighty
He who calls at our place of labor everyday
He who has passed beneath our sycamore tree
Saying "Come down, for today I must abide at your house"
May this great Comforter
This great Challenger of our spirit
May He challenge your spirit and mine
That we may not fail to gain the abundant Life. *Amen.*

Albert L. Reed

Prayer for Public Worship and Special Occasions

O Lord, Our God, we look to Thee as we begin this service. Be present in our midst and govern what we say and do, that both our words and our acts may be in accordance with Thy will.

Be very near to each of us, and may this be a day of rewarding meditation and service for Thee. *Amen.*

Rosalie M. Campbell

Dear God,

Enable us, we pray, to see your acts and to hear your voice amidst the rumbling and confusion of these earthquaking days. Equip us to seize the time that we may be vigilant in our freedom, committed in our callings, and just in our relations with all persons. *Amen.*

Devotions prayed in unison. Second Annual Convocation of Ministries to Blacks in Higher Education: April 29, 1971-May 1, 1971. William Walker, Student Leader, Gammon Theological Seminary.

Eternal Spirit,

In our best moments we realize that there must always be a place for the singing of angels in our lives—high moments when the sweeping winds of eternity surge through our souls, great moments when the stars of truth and love surround us, deep moments when we stand tiptoe to see what great things Thou has done.

Yet always we are tempted away from the singing of angels—our ears are deafened by ordinary sounds, our hearts are closed by the hates, our eyes are closed by the tinsel and glamor of life.

May this hour be one in which we are tempted upward by the singing of angels in every area of our lives. *Amen.*

M.L. Harvey

Prayer In The Black Tradition

O God, who hast called us to be Thy chosen people, forgive us our many imperfections and our unworthiness; purge us of those things which make it difficult or impossible to see Thy good works in us; be merciful unto us, O Lord, for our lack of responsibility to ourselves and to all. . . .

We praise Thy name for manifesting Thyself to us in Jesus Christ so that through Him we may know Thee more clearly. We thank Thee for Thy Church on earth, for all faithful people, and for the lives of the saints who have been before us. We honor Thee for the vision which many have seen or continue to see in working for reconciliation among people, and in striving for the visible unity of Thy divided church. We glorify Thee for all Thy manifold blessings. . . . We pray, O God, for strength that we may in all things seek to make Thy oneness known, and to demonstrate that in Christ all barriers such as race, kinship, and color have been broken down and are no more.

We pray Thee that we may have the courage to unfurl the banner of salvation which Thou hast given us, and that by lifting it up all men may know and worship Thee, through Jesus Christ, Thy Son, our Lord. *Amen.*

Bola Ige in *The Student at Prayer,* compiled by H.D. Bollinger.

Eternal God,
   We thank you that you've permitted us to get together to lift up your name. We thank you, O God, because you *are* God, and besides you there's no other. And you've been so good to us—better to us than we've ever been to ourselves. We are grateful, O God, because you're still in control. The sun still rises in the east and sets in the west. The wind still blows gentle and the storms still rise in their

Prayer for Public Worship and Special Occasions

time. You can still hold up your hands and the winds obey. You can still say, "Peace be still." Even the angels in heaven rejoice.

So we are grateful because you've been our all and all. We've been able to come this far by faith, leaning on the Lord.

We thank Thee, O God, because one day you saw fit to send your Son, Jesus, Mary's baby, the immaculate lamb of God, to take away the sins of the world. When our souls were dropping at the gates of hell, you made Jesus earth. He dwelt among us; he held our glory and the glory of the only begotten Son. Then on Calvary's cross he hung high and was stretched wide, and He never said a mumbalin' word, and died there for three hours for our sins and they buried him in a tomb. But we thank you, O God, that early in the morning your Son got up from the grave and said, "O death, where is thy sting? O grave, where is thy victory?"

We want to thank you because you brought peace. You gave us joy. *We want to thank you because you brought peace. You gave us joy.* We rejoice in the risen Christ— that we can gather and tell somebody that Jesus lives. Jesus is still real and I can feel it in my soul.

We thank you, O God, for all you've done for us and the church. We pray, O God, for the United Methodist Church. We know, O God, that we join in the history of the past. We recognize the struggles of the past. We look forward to the future, for we know it's you, O God, that holds the future in your hand. Reagan may be in the White House, but we know you're still on the throne. We don't have to fear and tremble though we walk through the valley of the shadow of death, for you said, "Walk together, children. There's a great camp meeting in the old campground."

Sometimes we get discouraged, and we think our work's in vain, but then the Holy Spirit revives my soul again. There's a balm in Gilead that makes the wounded whole. (O, thank you, Jesus.) There's a balm in Gilead that heals the sinsick soul.

We want to thank you because you've come by to tell us to look up. Somebody may be lost. O, Holy Spirit, come and with the quickening of your flesh, breathe upon us. Make us new creatures in Christ Jesus. Shake us up where we haven't been shaken. Take the old out and put in the new. Where there's jealousy, give us love. Where there's envy, give us peace. Where there's division, bring us back together again.

After while, when it's all over, somebody's going to sing on the other side, "I've got shoes; you've got shoes; all of God's children got shoes. And when I get to heaven gonna' put on my shoes and gonna' walk around heaven all day."

And while the choir and elders and holy angels sing, I want to hear you say, "Well done, my good and faithful servant." *Amen.*

Claude Edmonds. *Invocation prayer at 1981 Black Methodist for Church Renewal meeting in Philadelphia. Service at Tindley Temple. The prayer was undergirded with a musical background. It followed congregational singing of "We'll Understand It Better By and By."*

Eternal Spirit,
Who doth make the handiwork of the morning and the evening to rejoice, Who crowns our days with goodness, and Who looks on all the children of men with love, with grateful hearts we praise Thy majesty and power.

We give Thee thanks: for the inbreaking light that changes our earthly journey into a pilgrimage of greatness and glory; for the hallowed memories of human love and friendship that enrich the gladness of our lives; for the assurance that we do not walk alone within the awful vastness of the mystery that surrounds us, but that Thou art

Prayer for Public Worship and Special Occasions

with us, that Thy love is around us and Thy hand is upon us leading us onward toward an unknown greatness yet to be revealed.

O Thou whose redeeming love is our hope—deliver our lives from darkness and lead us into the freedom of those who find delight in the doing of Thy will.

In this hour together—deliver us from the blighting sin of imaginary goodness that prompts us to think more highly of ourselves than we ought to think and leaves us unmindful of the abounding goodness and kindness of our fellowmen.

Set our feet on mountain tops—grant us grace and bravery for the living of our lives.

In Jesus' name. *Amen.*

M.L. Harvey

Lord,

Teach us to understand the power of Thy presence and the gift of Thy blessings.

We are spiritually hungry and the bread of life is here.

We are thirsty and living waters are flowing by and through this place.

We are faltering amid life's treacherous currents, and the Rock of Ages is beneath our feet.

Grant unto us now strength for life's burdens and difficulties and on our troubled spirits bring the calm of Thine abiding peace this day and in the days to come. *Amen.*

M.L. Harvey

Almighty God,

Source of our being and Guide of our pilgrim journey, we turn from our feverish days to the calm of this experience to find the REAL meaning of life.

Forgive us, O God of Mercy, the fretfulness, the strain, and the vain purpose of our lives. We have turned our faces from the vision splendid as though Thou had not given us eyes. We are impatient as though there was no eternity. We have been desperate as though there was no hope in Christ. We have toiled for things that tarnish and spurned the gifts that are eternal.

Bid us, Our Father, as we lift our eyes from our valleys to Thy hills, that we may gain fresh knowledge and renewed courage for the living of these days. *Amen.*

M.L. Harvey

We bring ourselves to attention in Thy presence, Eternal Father, as those who find in Thee the whence and why and whither of their lives. Our flirtations and affairs with gods of our own making and our attempts to find abiding satisfaction in the train of passing circumstance leave us in the end all the more intent on knowing and loving Thee.

We acclaim the goodness that assigned us life and gave it to us wrapped in freedom:

The wisdom that made us different from one another so that the needs of one might interlock with the resources of his neighbor, completing both;

The providence that stays our folly in crisis moments when human judgement falters:

The grace that refreshes like a spring rain when the burden of our sin is more than we can bear.

It is alike our duty and our joy to offer Thee our thanks, O God. Through Jesus Christ Our Lord. *Amen.*

O Thou, Whose love goes out in unabated fullness to all the sons of men, hear us as we pray for those in our society who undergo the pain of adjusting to the unfamiliar:

Those in the hospital for the first time;
Those who are "breaking in" on a new job;
The aged mother recently admitted as a guest in a retirement home;
Parents responding to the discovery of a son or daughter on drugs;
The recently divorced;
The recently bereaved;
The recently paroled;
The recently convicted.

O Thou, Who abidest the same above the changes and chances of our hurrying years, be near to all who need Thee as they have the new; and let the comfort, pardon and direction of Thy Good News in Christ meet them and lead them on. Through Jesus Christ Our Lord. *Amen.*

O God, the hope of all who seek Thee and the joy of all who find Thee, move in our hearts who gather now before Thee.
Some of us are low and need the lifting word.
Some of us are high and need to be brought low.
Some of us are angry with the world.
Some of us are not angry enough.
Some of us are certain about too much.
Some of us are certain about too little.

O Thou, Who knowest every man for what he is and what he might become, bless each with what he needs the most, to the end that together we might better do Thy bidding.

All which we pray, grateful for a Saviour's love. Through Jesus Christ Our Lord. *Amen.*

M.L. Harvey

O God, Creator, Redeemer, Sanctifier,
Have mercy on us.

Prayer In The Black Tradition

For your love and continuing presence among us,
We thank you, O Lord.
For the many men and women who have been willing to risk because they trusted in you,
We thank you, O Lord.
For Abraham and Frederick Douglass and other men and women throughout the ages whose faith has been strong,
We thank you, O Lord.
For parents and teachers and friends who believe in us and are willing to help and support us when our faith grows weak,
We thank you, O Lord.
That we may be willing to risk and dare in your name,
We pray to you, Lord God.
That we may always be mindful of your loving presence and care,
We pray to you, Lord God.
Let us commend ourselves and one another to God.
To you, O Lord our God. Amen.

From *Free to Choose* by Mary Adebonojo.

Eternal God, Our Father,
    so high we cannot climb over Thee,
    so low we cannot go under Thee,
    so wide we cannot go around Thee,
    so we must come in through the door of prayers.
We thank Thee for all Thy gifts to us:
    for health and strength,
    for work and play,
    for this goodly fellowship through worship and service.
    We thank Thee for the beauty of the earth.
    We thank Thee for wonders of Thy universe.

Prayer for Public Worship and Special Occasions

We thank Thee for opportunities to serve this present age.
We pray for Thy children everywhere in the world.
May they be strengthened by Thy Spirit in the inner-man.
We pray for those who are ill in body or in mind—help them sense that underneath are the everlasting arms.
We pray for this Thy church.

Help us to see that, as we seek Thy help, Thy strength and power, we will find ourselves saying, "Surely the Lord was in this place and we knew it not." *Amen.*

M.L. Harvey

O God, creator and preserver of all things, we are thankful that you have given us life and strength to see the light of this day. We acknowledge your goodness and love for all of your creation and especially for all humankind. You cause the sun to shine on the good and the bad among us and, by your grace, call all people to seek your righteousness.

Forbid, O Lord, that we should boast of our goodness, for we admit that we are all sinners, saved only by your grace. Grant us the will to glorify your name by our witness and service to others. Enable us to minister to the needs of the poor, the lonely, the unloved, and the lost. Empower us to comfort the sick and those in prison. Let your Holy Spirit dwell among those who live in far away places where life is a struggle and where injustice, persecution, fear and pain abound.

We humbly beseech you to grant wisdom and compassion to the leaders of our nation and all nations around the world. Incline all peoples toward peace with justice. Teach us all to "study war no more," but to obey the call of your prophet to "beat (our) swords into plowshares and (our) spears into pruning hooks."

Help us, O God, to be sensitive to the needs of all of your people. May we love as we are loved by you and may we be forgiven all our failures through the grace of Jesus Christ who gave of himself for our redemption. Amen.

Levi Miller

PRAYERS BEFORE THE SERMON

O God, our Father, we come now to delve into the truths of your Holy Word. We acknowledge our inability to do anything without you, for the journey into Thy Word is a long and deep chasm. The mountains are too high and the valleys are too low, but we know that if you will walk by our sides, we can be successful.

Remove from our hearts and our minds those things that are displeasing in Thy sight. Those things that could cause interruption in the communication between me and You—blot them out right now, that we will be able to worship You in spirit and in truth.

Speak to us, Lord Jesus, that we may be able to speak to these Thy waiting children.

It's our prayer in the name of the Father, Son, and Holy Spirit. Amen.

Leonard Charles Stovall

Prayer for Public Worship and Special Occasions

Lord,
I need you right now.
I need you to be with me at this point in time.
I need for you to keep me from being selfish.
Keep me from getting in the way of your Word.
I need you, Father, to support me and to let your spirit flow
   through me.
Let it not be my own will
Nor let it be my own words,
But Thine!
In the name of Jesus we pray. *Amen.*

Leonard Charles Stovall. *Prayer before morning meditation at National Black Methodist for Church Renewal meeting, 1980 in Atlanta, Ga.*

Now, Lord, despite the stammering imperfections of the speaker's speech and the glaring discrepancies in his character, grant that the monstrance of your Gospel may be lifted up. O Crucified and Risen Lord; send tongues of fire to preach Thy Word. *Amen.*

William B. McClain. *At a national workshop on the Church in Transitional Communities in San Francisco.*

Be in the fleeting word, our Father, the stumbling effort. Touch mind and heart and life, that as we move from this place into the way that we must take, we shall not be alone, but shall feel Thy Presence beside us, all the way. *Amen.*

From *The Growing Edge* by Howard Thurman

Spirit of the living God, fall afresh on us. Spirit of the living God, fall afresh on us, melt us, mold us, and make us. Spirit of the living God, please fall afresh on us. Touch,

Prayer In The Black Tradition

Dear Lord, this day, with Thy finger of love these cold, back-bitin', lyin', hypocritin' hearts of ours. Set them, O Lord, through the mystery of worship, on hallowed ground, that we, indeed this day, may worship Thee in Spirit and in Truth and be better persons as a result of this service. We need you. We can't make this journey by ourselves. So just now, Lord, we pray that the meditations of our hearts, and all of our thoughts, humbly may be acceptable in Thy sight, Thou who art our Lord and Strength and Redeemer for evermore. *Amen.*

LaVon Kincaid

CLOSING PRAYERS AND BENEDICTIONS

O, God, our Heavenly Father from whom all blessings flow, we thank Thee for Thy power and for Thy loving kindness toward us. Help us to glorify Thy name. Help us to thank and praise Thee with our whole being. Help us to tell others of the wonderous things Thou art doing for us. Give us grace to show our thankfulness in daily living. Help us to spend our lives in quietness and serene trust in Thee. Save us from fretfulness and worry. Restrain us from impatience. Make this day a season of new conquests and of fresh thanksgiving. We cannot see Thee but we do see Jesus, Thy Son. We receive His word, enjoy His fellowship, walk by His counsel and trust ourselves to the mystery of His cross. Abiding in Him may we have the assurance of Thy love. *Amen.*

Roscoe Conklin Williams

Prayer for Public Worship and Special Occasions

God, forgive us our hesitancy and fear,
    our almost believing,
    our almost daring,
    our almost going all the way.
Draw near to us,
    the better to press Thy claims upon us,
    the more clearly to evoke from us
    an unconditional "Yes!"
Through Jesus Christ Our Lord. *Amen.*

M.L. Harvey

Dear Father, we thank you for streams and brooks and rivers that never run dry. We thank you for your everlasting Word, for promising us that you will be with us always, even when we existentially are experiencing the ends of the earth. When we are thirsty, you promised to satiate that thirst. When we are hungry, you promised to feed us. And we come, and we move through this service with this same kind of confidence; hoping, longing to reach out to others struggling and grappling with these same sorts of things. May they appropriate it. May we be the instrument for this appropriation. *Amen.*

Edward Ducree. *This prayer closed a sermon delivered for a national Black Methodist for Church Renewal morning meditation on "What Do You Do When Your Well Runs Dry?"*

Dear Lord, teach us to know that thou art with us every day and every hour through trials and tribulations. May we have the assurance in our weakness, thou art our strength; in pain, our comfort; forsaken, our refuge. In the name of our Lord who suffered and died so that we might have life. *Amen.*

Willard A. Williams

Prayer In The Black Tradition

O God, our Father, all the confusion inspired by our weakness and our inadequacy and our failure we make as a part of our offering to Thee. What in us is dark, illumine. What is low, raise and support; that, in ways that we can understand, and in ways that transcend the limitations of our understanding, we may be living instruments in Thy hands. Do not let us separate from Thy Spirit, as we separate one from the other, but go with us, O God, go with us, our Father.

From *The Growing Edge* by Howard Thurman

May God ever bless, keep, guide and continue to prosper you in your uplifting work for humanity, be it great or small, is my daily prayer. And may those whom God has redeemed learn to walk and talk with him, not only daily and hourly, but momently, through the things that he has created. *Amen.*

W. Maurice King in *Soul and Soil*

We thank Thee, O Father, for the time that we have spent together. May we long be influenced by the inspiration we have received here. Bless us now and guide us day by day. *Amen.*

Rosalie M. Campbell

We are grateful, our Father, for the light which Thou dost cast upon our pathway, illuminating the deepest darkness in which our souls go astray. Dismiss us from this place, but leave us not, as we seek this day, and tomorrow, and tomorrow, and tomorrow, to find the way, the truth, and the life.

From *The Growing Edge* by Howard Thurman

Prayer for Public Worship and Special Occasions

With a certain sense of shame and limitation, but with enthusiasm of spirit, we make to Thee, O God, the offering of our minds and spirits. Be with us as we move each one of us into the pattern of the daily responsibility of life, and may nothing separate us from Thy love today, and tomorrow, and tomorrow, and tomorrow, O God, the Father of our spirits.

From *The Growing Edge* by Howard Thurman

Forgive us, our Father, for blindness, for pride and arrogance of mind, for the subtle conceit that undermines the integrity of all that we think and feel and do. Accept us, O God, as we are, and leave us not alone as we separate one from the other, but bless our days and our coming together again.

From *The Growing Edge* by Howard Thurman

The God of Hope and Love, the God of the One we call the Christ, the God who is the Father/Mother of all humankind, transform this moment into a sign of His Church; strengthen you in each endeavor and moment to cause your life to find new nerve and commitment.

James Lawson

God, grant that the words of our faith
    may become the attitudes of our
    minds and dispositions of our hearts.
Help us to be toward others
    what Thou hast been toward us,
    for the sake of Jesus Christ, our Lord. *Amen.*

M.L. Harvey

ALTAR PRAYERS

The altar prayer, whether before or after the sermon, is a special time in black worship. Both in America and Africa, the altar is likely to be filled with souls who, both figuratively and literally, are reaching out to God for the ministrations of His Spirit through the one who prays.

The altar prayer is a lively and dramatic form of the traditional collect of formal white worship. In the collect, the concerns or needs of the people are brought together, i.e., *collected* and offered to God. This may well occur in the altar prayer. It may be joined, affirmed, and appropriated by those worshipers kneeling at the altar by such expressions as: "Yes, Lord," "Jesus, have mercy," or "Thank you, Jesus." In services in which several ministers participate, it is an honor to be called on to pray the altar prayer. To do it with power and spirit is a gift from God.

The following account of "Black Harry" Hosier from *Harry Hosier: Circuit Rider* by Warren Thomas Smith, illustrates the force of prayer. The other prayers that follow also exhibit the special sense of purpose and meaning which the altar prayer holds for the black worshiper and those who have learned to worship in the black tradition.

George Raybold told of Hosier's being assigned to the Trenton Circuit in 1803 "in company with" John Walker (1764–1849), who recalled a highly charged situation:

> On one occasion, at an appointment at Hackettstown, there was a lady in the house where the preachers stayed who declared "she would not hear the black." Harry heard it, and retired into a corner of the garden, and prayed in great fervour, until the hour of meeting. At the conclusion of the sermon, Harry arose, stood behind the chair, and began, in the most humble manner, to speak of sin as a disease; all were affected there, and the Lord had

sent a remedy by the hands of a physician; but, alas! he was black! and some might reject the only means of cure, because of the hands by which it was sent to them that day.

Hosier logically built his theme. He went on in the same strain, until all hearts were moved; then he prayed, (few had the gift of prayer as had Black Harry; he was like Bishop Asbury in this respect—awful, powerful, and overwhelming!) The moment had come for the traditional altar call—call to the mourner's bench—and "a great time" it was. The "lady was cut to the heart, and speedily converted, as were many others, on that memorable occasion."

This (morning)) our Heavenly Father, once more and again you have spared a few of your children another chance to be out to the house of worship one more time.

You watched over us last night while we slumbered and slept. You kept our couch from becoming our tomb, woke us up this morning, clothed in our right mind, and with a reasonable amount of health and strength. You have promised that where two or three of your children gather together in your name, that you would be in the midst.

"O Thou by whom we come to God, the Life, the Truth, the way; the path of prayer Thyself hast trod: Lord teach us how to pray." We come to you as empty pitchers to a fountain that shall never run dry. We are in need of a doctor, not of medicine which only has the power to cure the physical body and mind, but also a healer who can lay his nail-printed hands on our sin-sick souls and tell us to get up and walk.

We want to thank you Lord Jesus, because you have brought us a mighty long ways; you were our bread when we were hungry, our water in a dry and thirsty land, our shelter in the time of storm, our Lily of the Valley, our Bright and Morning Star, our Prince of Peace, our King of Kings, and Lord of Lords. The road has been stony and rocky, and with tears has been watered, but "God of our weary years, and God of our silent tears, Thou who hast by Thy might led us into the light, keep us forever in thy path we pray."

And when our task on earth is done, when by thy grace the victory's won, we pray that you will give us a home somewhere around your throne in a world that has no end. We pray in the name of Jesus Christ our Lord. *Amen.*

Glenn A. Brooks

O Lord, here we stand. We've heard the experience of Peter and John and then we've heard the experience of that John who was on the isle of Patmos and we see the handwriting on the wall. Times gonna get tough and, Lord, we've committed ourselves to the Kingdom. Tonight we want to rededicate. We want to rededicate, and say Lord, "Here am I; send me." Some folks may not like me, I may lose my job, I may be called first one thing and another, but Lord help me to know how to be wise. Don't make a fool out of me Lord, at least let me be a fool for Christ's sake.

Lord, teach us how to bear a witness. Teach us how to be sensitive. Teach us where we are to stop. We can't be everywhere; take us by our hands and lead us by the temples that you'd like us to stop by. And let us see the lame men and women that you would want us to help and then give us the strength to get up on our feet and declare with all that is within us that the Kingdoms of Jesus Christ will be the Kingdoms of this world.

Lord, help us. Help us, Lord. Help me, Lord. Help me in my post of duty. I'm a teacher, Lord; help me as a teacher. Lord, I'm a preacher, and sometimes the powers that urge me to compromise are very strong. But help me, Lord, to stand up for the Kingdom.

Prayer for Public Worship and Special Occasions

Lord, there are pastors here who are trying to serve, who are trying to love, who are not about anything radical, but now just to be a Christian, Lord, is making them to be viewed in a negative light. Lord, be with them. Be with them as they return with a dedication to your cause, and while we wait here, Lord, I don't know how you are gonna do it in these days. Some people have notions of how you annoint your people. Some want outward demonstrations, some want inward demonstrations, but, Lord, it matters not to me just that you come with us.

Lord, it matters not. Maybe fill us with the inward light and give us the powers of spirit that have lead the Quakers through the years to witness in trying times. Lord, give us a Pentocostal power to somehow clean out the carbon in our hearts that we might run with joy and enthusiasm. Lord, anyway you want to bless us; bless us quiet, Lord, or bless us noisy. Bless us with an inward penetration or with an outward demonstration. But however you do it, Spirit of the living God, fall afresh on each one of us. Lord, break up our kingdom. Melt down the fragments, then mold us Lord; and then fill us with the Spirit of the living God. Fall afresh upon us while we stand right here in this chapel tonight, do something for us. Do something for us that makes us know you're still real. Do something for us that lets us know we're not alone. Do something for us, Lord, that sends us on our way fully confident that the power of God is more than a match for the enemy.

Lord, sustain us, lead us, and guide us and when we get low, lift us and when we get wrong, correct us. And when we go out on the deep end, give us a life raft to bring us back to the shore. But Lord, be with us and stand by us and your name which is worthy shall have all the praise, for we ask these blessings in the name of the One whose Kingdom shall have no end. *Amen.*

James A. Forbes, Jr. *Duke University Chapel, October 24, 1978*

Our Father,

We come before Thine altar to remember anew that we are members of the human race whom Thou hast created and sustained through all these years. Help us to recognize that above and beyond the accidents of climate and geography and culture—we have an essential kinship with all Thy children everywhere.

That as members of the only race Thou dost recognize, we have the capacity to love beauty, to live according to reason, to commit ourselves to high and lofty purposes, and to serve Thy children in truth and justice.

In these moments make us aware of the occasions when we have acted in the light of accidents of race and creed and culture; help us to seek Thy forgiveness for these errors of ommission and commission and lift our hearts and minds to our true stature as Thy sons and Thy daughters. For we pray in the name of the Father of us all. *Amen.*

M.L. Harvey

Our Father and Our God,

We come now to ask that your healing power will come upon all of these thy children.

What ever the problem is, Heavenly Father, we pray that you will answer it: where there's sickness—we pray that you will bring about health; where there's loneliness—we pray that you will bring comfort; where there is hate—we pray that you usher in love.

We need you this morning, Heavenly Father. We want you to come by this church. Fill us with joy divine and reverence and make a home here with us.

We pray that you give us that love that comes from heart to heart and from breath to breath.

Teach us to love our neighbors. Teach us to be concerned about our neighbors. Teach us to walk in the ways of purity. Teach us to walk in the way that is straight so that in the end, when you return, we will be able to stand before you, and you will say to us, "Well done—Well done—Well done, my good and faithful servant. You've been faithful over a few things, but I'll make you ruler over many." We are looking forward to the day when we can go to that big review because—won't be no more sickness—won't be no more sorrow—won't be no more heart breaks—everything will be made right.

Whatever the need—whatever our problem—to the deaf, hearing will return—heal the blind man one day—heal a man that couldn't walk one day—heal the little girl who has been dead one day. Great Father—you can heal if we ask you and if we believe it. You are able to heal.

In Jesus' name—In Jesus' name we pray. *Amen.*

Frank L. Horton, *First United Methodist Church, Monrovia, Liberia, West Africa, 1982*

Eternal God, whose days are without end and whose mercies cannot be numbered, we give Thee our humble and heartfelt thanks for the world which Thou hast prepared and furnished for our dwelling place. We thank Thee for the rising and setting suns, for seed time and harvests, for summer and winter, and for daily comforts which minister to our lives.

Help us to be grateful for the manifold ways in which Thou dost bless us, move us to express our thanks to Thee, for life and for the days of our years. But above all, O God, we thank Thee for Thyself and for the wonder and majesty of Thy love that will not let us go. A love that touches our lives even when we are unaware of it, a love that shames us in our unworthiness and yet moves us to a nobler living, a love always ready to receive us when we wander from our Father's House. Speak to our needs this day.

Where there is sorrow, bring comfort.
Where there is fear, give assurance.
Where there is loneliness, offer companionship.
Where there is illness, rest Thy healing hand.
Where there is guilt, offer forgiveness.
Where there is discouragement, bring hope.

Lift us, Father, out of ourselves as we gaze upon Thy matchless beauty and send us forth strengthened by Thy Spirit, through Jesus Christ our Lord. *Amen.*

Found by Elmira Higgins in her mother's papers.

PRAYERS FOR SPECIAL OCCASIONS

Several contributors have provided comments or prayers for group occasions. These are not necessarily meant for the worship service, but for the service of worshipers. The same characteristics and qualities that mark prayer in the worship setting are manifestly present here as well. Also included in this section are prayers for special situations or occasions which most likely will be observed by the worshiping community.

Our Heavenly Father, we need not tell Thee that we are here. We are fully in Thy sight and are all known to Thee. And so we come in this opening session of the Conference to gather at Thy feet, to look into Thy face and to submit and commit ourselves and the program for the entire months to be and so we ask Thee to come not in the

Prayer for Public Worship and Special Occasions

mornings only but through every hour of the day of the entire Conference sessions to be with every delegate and with everybody here, so that the work of this Conference may be done through us by Thee, so that when we have closed the Conference, the people may be able to say, "The Lord has been here: The Lord has done great things." We come to consecrate ourselves anew to Thee. We come to bind ourselves to the great and small tasks that lie before us. Thou art attempting still to redeem this world and to bring it to Christ. Much has been done and much remains to be done. Help us not to be fainthearted in the task. We are not machines. We are workers and we come asking Thee to use the best that is in us as Thou wilt that we may do our part in saving the world. Problems are confronting us that were not here the other day and that we were not asked to confront: but we are asked today to confront them. Help us to answer. Help us to witness, a witness for Thee and be instruments in Thy hands so that people may know that Thou art through us still redeeming the world. May folks, through us, find out Thou art still in the business of saving men. May folks find out that we have a relationship with Christ and that we have a vicarious atonement, that can cleanse from all sin. And help us to work with Thee that through us Thou shall do a mighty work. Clean up the world. Clear out all the saloons everywhere. Wipe our flag clean from all signs of war and may it be a signal of peace and a new paradise everywhere that men may walk and not be afraid.

Speak loudly to us Lord, and bless us in all things for Christ's sake. "Our Father who art in Heaven." *Amen.*

Charles Albert Tindley. *Delivered at the 1924 General Conference of The Methodist Church.*

O Lord God, we ask as the days unfold, many issues lifted and discussed, much planning made, and done, may this network be strengthened and enriched. Help us to be aware of your care and of the needs about us. May we daily see ways in which the church may become that extended family of love, care, and compassion, so that we become aware, that we may see that vision which keeps us, on this side of slavery, and moves us toward that promised land where despair is becoming dignity, fear—faith, and there is an end to the destruction of community. Amen.

James Lawson. *Opening Worship. National Urban Ministry Network Leaders Meeting, Los Angeles, May, 1983*

Eternal God, spare us the folly of hiding from Thee
   behind tight schedules and closed minds.
Give us the venturesomeness that belongs to faith.
   the humility to revise ourselves and our opinions,
   and the joy of discovery.
     Through Jesus Christ our Lord. *Amen.*

M.L. Harvey

Church School Staff Prayer before Meeting Classes on Sunday Morning

Our Gracious Heavenly Father, we approach thy throne this morning with hearts of gratitude and a spirit of love. As we prepare ourselves this morning to meet our classes, we pray for more wisdom, more understanding and a renewed commitment to be willing to sacrifice ourselves in our efforts to present Thy teachings to all of our classes. Help us to learn how to teach through example as well as precepts. Cleanse us from all selfish ideas so that we may be fit to present Thy truths to all entrusted in our leadership and guidance. Bless our Sunday School;

and we pray for Thy continued love which abounds and with grateful hearts we will give Thee the praises through Jesus Christ our Lord. *Amen.*

Morris L. Woodson

Prayer for the Choir on Sunday Morning before the Processional

Eternal God our Father, Thou in whose presence our very souls take delight, we thank Thee for this another day and another opportunity which we have to lift our voices in song in singing praises to Thy glorious name. We pray this morning for Thy divine presence and the visitation of the Holy Spirit. As we lift our voices in song, we pray that Thou will keep us ever mindful that we are not singing for personal gratification but rather we are trying to make use of that talent which Thou gavest us to the glory of our worship service. Help us to grow in unity for in unity there is strength. Bless our choir according to the blessing that Thou see we stand in need of and as we go into the service this morning, we pray that our singing will lift some heart that was heavy; renew somebody's strength; will build hope into the seemingly hopeless; and cause somebody to make up his or her mind to follow Jesus. These and other blessings we ask in Thy name. *Amen.*

Rosalie M. Campbell

Prayer for a Committee

O, Father, grant wisdom and give direction to those who serve on this committee; may they work harmoniously and effectively. Show them Thy will, and move them to concerted action to achieve it. Give them open minds, warm, responsive hearts, and a united purpose.

Help them to realize that they are your representatives; and may they seek to take such action as will be good for all. We ask in Jesus' name. *Amen.*

Rosalie M. Campbell

Student Day Prayers

Lord, we are grateful that You have given us the ability to learn. We are glad that, on your earth, we may ask not only "what" but "why." We thank You that we are ever in search of newer knowledge and better understanding of this world and our roles in it. We pray that our quest for knowledge is a quest not only to know the facts of our world but the truths of our existence. We pray that we interpret what our minds perceive with what our hearts believe. In this world of awesome sciences and wonderous humanities, we ask Your guidance that we may never forget the Creator and Author of all that this world holds to be explored, explained, and understood. In Your name. *Amen.*

Betty Hart

Lord God of our fathers, who hast chosen to remain unknown even while from the very beginning of creation making Thyself known, readily do we kneel before Thee in worship and adoration. Emblazon us with the strickening character of Thy love that, being tossed about, we may with all vigor recognize Thee as He upon whom the concreteness of our situation depends.

Permeate our present learning with the constant awareness that always we stand before Thee, and that this posture hallows both our acquiring and our using of that which we gain here. May we with involvement of heart, toil of mind, and wholeness of strength make known to our university community who Thou art and how Thou hast reliably performed in and through Jesus Christ for the redemption of all life. It is by the grace of the Christ event we pray. *Amen.*

James Lawson in *The Student at Prayer,* compiled by H.D. Bollinger.

Offertory Prayers

Lord, these gifts are but symbols of our commitment to you as evidenced by our service through ministries of your church. *Amen.*

Levi Miller

O Lord, we offer to you ourselves in gratitude for your saving grace. The symbols of this offering represent only a portion of our commitment to your will for humankind. *Amen.*

Levi Miller

A Liturgy for Celebrating the Eucharist

Celebrant: Father, we give you thanks for what we are: Black, proud, and determined people who have been refined in the bitter fire of slavery. And we give you thanks for giving us the sight to see a movement. A movement that cannot be stopped by all the forces of oppression. We give thanks for setting an unshakeable example of what it means to be fully human. You showed us that to be fully human means

you are never satisfied as long as one of your brothers is oppressed. That as long as one person is not free no one is free.
You showed us that we must fight for that freedom and that we can't let nothing or no one "turn us around."

ALL: So we say, "Right On!" to you, Lord, for being the one to show us that nothing can stop the truth.
> They can lock it up,
> They can beat it,
> They can distort it,
> They can label it,
> They can out-number it,
> They can out-maneuver it,

but no matter what they try to do, that truth will make us free, and even those who seek to destroy it will be defeated by it.

Celebrant: And so as a free Black people, we stand up and raise our fists toward the heavens, not in anger, but in the salute to the God who made us Black (with more shades than the rainbow), proud and beautiful. We say:

All: HOLY! HOLY! HOLY!
Lord God of all Creation.
Heaven and earth are filled with your Glory!
We bless your name.
Blessed is he who comes in the name of the Lord!

Celebrant: Father, we pray that we may never again lose sight of who we are, and what we are about. We pray that we may develop an undying love for each other. For it is only

Prayer for Public Worship and Special Occasions

through love that we will ever get ourselves together. But a love that demands you impress on anyone who seeks to oppress you, the fact that you are a man and a woman, an equal part of God's creation. And you will do all that is necessary to bring that fact to light.

As we offer to you this bread and wine, we offer ourselves to each other.

Take our bread, take our wine, take our lives, so that we can get on with the business at hand. For we all know, Father, what time it is.

The Absalom Jones Association of the Episcopal Church at Howard University, Washington, D.C.

Prayers of Thanks

Thanks be to Thee for all the interior resources of power by which the spirit—even in the midst of the tumult and confusion—can nobly live.

Thanks be to Thee for the inward shepherding which can lead us in green pastures and beside still water, restoring the soul.

We thank Thee for the fellowship we enjoy with kindred minds. With gratitude, we lift in Thy presence the remembrance of our friends. In our imaginations we see their faces; in our minds we think their names. For their comfort in days of trouble,
    stability in time of confusion,
    guidance when we were bewildered,
    inspiration when we were downcast,
gracing our lives with beauty and crowning them with joy, thanks be to Thee.

Be Thou our God according to our need and send us

forth from this place saying, "Bless the Lord, O my soul and all that is within me, bless His holy name. *Amen.*

M.L. Harvey

O God, Creator, Redeemer, Sanctifier,
Have mercy on us.
For your love and continuing presence among us,
We thank you, O Lord.
For insuring our survival as a people and for being with us in our continuing struggle for liberation from all that would diminish our stature as human beings,
We thank you, O Lord.
For all men, women, and children who work for justice, liberation, and peace,
We thank you, O Lord.
That we may see you at work in our lives and history,
We pray to you, Lord God.
That we may join with Christ and with those who have gone before us to work for justice, liberation, and peace.
We pray to you, Lord God.
Glory to God whose power, working in us, can do infinitely more than we can ask or imagine; glory be to him from generation to generation in the church and in Christ Jesus for ever and ever. *Amen.* (cf. Ephesians 3:20-21)

From *Free to Choose* by Mary Adebonojo

A Thanksgiving Poem

The sun hath shed its kindly light,
   Our harvesting is gladly o'er,
Our fields have felt no killing blight,
   Our bins are filled with goodly store.

Prayer for Public Worship and Special Occasions

From pestilence, fire, flood, and sword
   We have been spared by thy decree,
And now with humble hearts, O Lord,
   We come to pay our thanks to thee.

We feel that had our merits been
   The measure of thy gifts to us,
We erring children, born of sin,
   Might not now be rejoicing thus.

No deed of ours hath brought us grace;
   When thou wert nigh our sight was dull,
We hid in trembling from thy face,
   But thou, O God, wert merciful.

Thy mighty hand o'er all the land
   Hath still been open to bestow
Those blessings which our wants demand
   From heaven, whence all blessings flow.

Thou hast, with ever watchful eye,
   Looked down on us with holy care,
And from thy storehouse in the sky
   Hast scattered plenty everywhere.

Then lift we up our songs of praise
   To thee, O Father, good and kind;
To thee we consecrate our days;
   Be thine the temple of each mind.

With incense sweet our thanks ascend;
   Before thy works our powers pall;
Though we should strive years without end,
   We could not thank thee for them all.

Paul Laurence Dunbar

Lord of lords, Creator of all things, God of all things,
  God over all gods, God of sun and rain,
    You created the earth with a thought and us with
      Your breath.
Lord, we brought in the harvest. The rain watered the
    earth,
  the sun drew cassava and corn out of the clay. Your
  mercy showered blessing after blessing over our country. Creeks grew into rivers; swamps became lakes. Healthy fat cows graze on the green sea of the savanna. The rain smoothed out the clay walls, the mosquitoes drowned in the high waters.
Lord, the yam is fat like meat, the cassava melts on the
    tongue,
  oranges burst in their peels, dazzling and bright.
Lord, nature gives thanks, Your creatures give thanks.
  Your praise rises in us like the great river.
Lord of lords, Creator, Provider, we thank you.
  In the name of Jesus Christ. *Amen.*

From "I Sing Your Praise All Day Long" in *Young Africans at Prayer*

O God, it is comforting to know that I cannot go beyond or below or around You, for You are everywhere. You bring comforting faith to man, whether he be on Manhattan or on the moon, in the Bronx or in the boondocks. Thank You, God, for Your universal love. Thanks, again and again. *Amen.*

W. Maurice King in *Soul and Soil*

Christmas Prayers

O Lord God, here we are with our hopes and fears. Grant that out of our Christmas celebration some gift of insight might come so that, having affirmed Jesus as Lord, we may go forth with confidence and hope. Through his name we pray, and in his power we live. *Amen.*

James A. Forbes, Jr. in *Outstanding Black Sermons: Volume 3*

Almighty God and Heavenly Father, with a joyful heart, we pause to say thank you for the privilege of celebrating and sharing another Christmastide; the Birthday of our Lord Jesus Christ.

We offer praise to Thee, for the Immaculate Conception; for Jesus' Mission and Ministry of Mercy; for His propitiatory Sacrifice on Calvary's Cross, that we might be saved, and adopted as heirs in the family of God through His crucifixion and Resurrection.

We rejoice in the thought and fact, that Christmas-day reminds us of God's promised Kingdom-day; when Jesus shall return again to earth with us to reign as King of King and Lord of Lord. As the Psalmist shouted, "The Lord of Hosts, He is the King of Glory."

Bless us to this Christmas and make us a blessing to the Christ of Christmas. *Amen.*

R.W. Cunningham

A Wedding Benediction

Our Eternal God, Creator and Preserver of all mankind, the Giver of all spiritual grace, the Author of life everlasting; please send Thy blessing upon these Thy servants, this man and this woman, whom we now bless in Thy name; that as Isaac and Rebekah of old, lived faithfully together, so may these two persons, perform and keep the vow and covenant made between them in this hour of sacred ceremony.

May these vows and spirit of love deepen and sustain this man and this woman through the vicissitudes of life, and may peace, joy, and happiness be theirs through Jesus Christ our Lord. *Amen.*

R.W. Cunningham

Commemoration Prayer at a Funeral

Eternal Spirit:
   From Whom we come
   To Whom we belong
   And in Whose service is life's meaning
   Our first word is one of thanksgiving for Thy servant who lived among us for more than fourscore years, and has now moved to the church triumphant.
   We thank Thee for the life she lived
   For her sense of what was vital
   For her wide range of interests in the problems of this community,
   For the loves of her life—this church fellowship, her profession, her family, the organizations to which she belonged . . .
   For her passionate interest in persons who needed and could use her assistance.
   Let Thy mercy rest upon us, a company of her friends who today remember with grateful affection Thy servant, who has moved from the seen to the unseen world.
   Give especially to those who most intimately mourn her going, wide margins of comfort around their spiritual need, and deep wells of strength from which to draw their consolation, as they remember with joy the life they shared with her.
   Thou art the God of the living. With Thee there is no death. Our departed one is at home with Thee for evermore. As Thou didst not lose her in her coming to us, so we have not lost her in her return to Thee. Deepen in us this faith in life eternal.
   Once more we stand upon the shore of a rimless sea,

Prayer for Public Worship and Special Occasions

and bid farewell to a ship that loses itself over the horizon of our world. As we stand upon this nearer shore and bid farewell, grant us faith to hear the triumphant voices which on yonder shore cry to her
"WELCOME" and "ALL HAIL"
"For all thy saints who from their labors rest,
Who Thee by faith before the world confessed,
Thy name, O Jesus, be forever blest."
ALLELUIA.

M.L. Harvey. *Commemoration prayer at the funeral of Mary Rayford Collins, M.L. Harvey's mother-in-law.*

A Funeral Invocation

Our Heavenly Father, we come unto Thee in this time of sorrow, acknowledging our utter dependence upon Thee. We know Thou dost love us, and doest all things well; and that Thou canst turn even this shadow of death into light of morning. Comfort our saddened hearts, and help us now as we reverently submit our hearts and hope unto Thee.

Thou art our Refuge and Strength, a very pleasant help in this time of our trouble. Give us Thy strength and mercy. May we, who mourn today find real comfort and balm of healing in Thy sustaining Grace. This we humbly pray in Jesus' name. *Amen.*

R.W. Cunningham

Martin Luther King, Jr.

The Reverend Ronald English prayed the following prayer at the funeral of Dr. Martin Luther King, Jr. Because of its powerful response to a tragic moment in history and its deep theological content, we include it as the conclusion to this gathering of Prayers for Public Worship and Special Occasions.

Let us bow our heads in a moment of solemn utterance.
Eternal and everlasting God Our Father.

The height of our aspirations, the depth of our existence, Thou who art the giver and sustainer of life, from Whom all things have come and to Whom all things shall return, we beseech Thy comforting presence in this hour of deepest bereavement.

For our hearts are heavily laden with sorrow and remorse at the removal of one of history's truest representatives of Thy will and purpose for mankind.

While we pray for comfort we pray for wisdom to guide our thoughts aright at this hour. For we, O God, in our limited vision cannot begin to comprehend the full significance of this tragic occurrence.

And so we raise the perennial question of Job: "Why?" as we weep for the moment.

Yet we are reminded by the best of the Christian tradition that in the total economy of the universe good will ultimately triumph. Though sorrow tarries for the night, joy comes in the morning.

We know, O God, that even in this little while of sorrow we need not weep for the deceased, for here was one man truly prepared to die.

In his last hours he testified himself that he had been to the mountaintop, that his eyes had seen the glory of the coming of the Lord. We know he had no fear of death.

Help us to find consolation in the fact that his life was a gift given to us at this crucial juncture in our history out of the graciousness of Thy being.

And so we had no real claims upon him. In the fullness of time he has gone. He knew where he came from and he knew where he was going.

And so as we abide in this knowledge our gratitude will abate our sorrows.

We know, O God, that life is but a moment in eternity and that he who lives for the moment will surely die, yet he who lives for eternity and dedicates his life to those ultimate principles of truth, justice and love as this man has done will never die.

Inspire us to accept the imperative that his life so full exemplifies—that we would not judge the worth of our lives by their physical longevity, but by the quality of their service to mankind.

He has shown us how to live, O God. He has shown us how to love. Yet the manner of his being was so strange and unfamiliar in our world, a world that abounds in war, hatred and racism, a world that exhalts the wicked and crucifies the righteous, a world where a world of condemnation is familiar while a word of kindness is strange.

So this man was a peculiar man. He taught a peculiar teaching. So he was not of this world. So in the course of human events the forces of time, faith and the hopes of the oppressed converged upon a single man.

Though once in a century the midwife of oppression snatches from the womb of history a child of destiny, the record of events testifies to the fact that history cannot bear the truth.

We have witnessed the life of the crucified Christ and we have seen the slaying of Martin Luther King. So like a wild carnivorous beast that turns upon its own and devours them, history has turned once more because it could not bear the truth that he spoke or the judgment that he brought.

And so, like Jesus, not only did Martin Luther King challenge the status quo, but he challenged our mode of existence. Therefore, like Jesus, he had to die as a martyr for a cause that challenged the world's assumed posture of security.

The light came into the darkness but the darkness knew it not.

Oh God, our leader is dead. And so now the question that he posed during his life finds us in all its glaring

Prayer In The Black Tradition

proportions: "Where do we go from here? Chaos or community."

We pray, O merciful Father, that the removal of this man will not nullify the revelation given through him.

Undergird our feeble efforts with Thy strength and renew our courage to devote the full weight of our being to the ideas that he has thus far so nobly advanced.

Deepen our commitment to nonviolence so that this country will not be run asunder by a frustrated segment of the black masses who would blaspheme the name of Martin Luther King by commiting violence in his name.

Grant that the Congress and President of this nation who have been so generous and gracious in their memorial tributes will be guided by the memory of this suffering servant and return to the legislative halls determined to pass without compromise or reservations legislations so vitally needed to preserve domestic tranquility and prevent social disruption.

Grant, O lover of peace, that we will effectively negotiate for a peaceful settlement in Vietnam to end the brutal slayings and communal atrocities committed in the names of democracy.

Tune our hearts, O God, to hear and respond to the echoes of this undying voice of the ages, a voice of love and reconciliation in the present, a voice of hope and confidence in the future.

Grant that in response to his sacrificial death we will work toward that day when the long and tragic tune of man's inhumanity to man will resolve into a chorus of peace and brotherhood. Then love will tread out the baleful sighs of anger and in its ashes plant a tree of peace.

This is our prayer. Grant us thy gracious benediction. Amen.

3

PRAYER FOR PERSONAL DEVOTIONS

The black religious experience is marked by a sense of community or corporateness and church has special meaning to the black worshiper. But personal prayer also has great value and meaning.

Mrs. Thelma S. Dixon recalls:

> Ever since childhood my parents taught us to pray—in the morning, giving table blessings, at night. Upon graduation we knelt to pray in thanks to God because those were very tough times, depression days. So we were taught "in everything give thanks." When I had to take tests, I prayed. Then when I got my teaching job we all knelt in prayer. Because of my parents' example that has kept me on an even keel. I also cannot forget my grandmothers. When I would become discouraged, "Mama" Scott would sing to me, "Count Your Blessings." But I do pray for others as well as myself. I remember once when I was ill from a heart attack, I began to tremble all over for no apparent reason. The only way out I knew was to pray. I just told God, I had been so busy praying for others I had forgotten about me. So please heal me. The cure was instant! My mother said she knew something had taken place because there was a sudden calmness in the room. I try to live close

to God that others may be able to be better Christians because of dealing with me.

There is a striking similarity to the words of a slave recorded in *Lay My Burden Down: A Folk History of Slavery.*

> I'm puny and no 'count. Ain't able to do much. But I was crippled. I had a hurting in my leg, and I couldn't walk without a stick. Finally, one day I went to go out and pick some turnips. I was visiting my son in Palestine. My leg hurt so bad that I talked to the Lord about it. And it seemed to me, He said, "Put down your stick." I put it down, and I ain't used it since. God is a momentary God. God knowed what I wanted and He said, "Put down that stick," and I ain't been crippled since. It done me so much good. Looks like to me when I get to talking about the Lord, ain't nobody a stranger to me.

Other comments and observations underscore the importance of prayer for individual believers. Often, as Thelma Dixon expressed earlier, the gift of prayer was learned at the feet of others. Glenn A. Brooks puts it succinctly:

> I grew up partially in the home of an Aunt of mine. She and her husband believed in a strong prayer life. They had family prayer and Bible verses before breakfast, before retiring for bed, and always before taking a trip some place. It was there that the hymn, "Prayer is the soul's sincere desire," became a favorite of mine. The focus was on "the simplist form of speech . . . the Christian's vital breath," and the way we come to God.

George Washington Carver had a significant sense of the purpose and power of prayer. "For quite some time I have lived on prayer, beef suet and corn meal, being at the last without the suet and meal." In *Soul and Soil,* W. Maurice King quotes Carver as saying:

> My prayers seem to be more of an attitude than anything else. I indulge in very little lip service, but ask the Great

Creator silently, daily, and often many times a day, to permit me to speak to Him through the three great Kingdoms of the world which He has created—the animal, mineral, and vegetable Kingdoms—to understand their relations to each other, and our relations to them and to the Great God who made all of us. I ask Him daily and often momently to give me wisdom, understanding, and bodily strength to do His will; hence I am asking and receiving all the time.

The following statement by Levi Miller speaks powerfully about prayer as "profoundly personal."

Prayer is a way of life authenticated only in the conscious effort to realize God's inescapable presence and involvement in every aspect of life-experiences. Life in all its form and expressions is God's creation and though I cannot apprehend his purpose in all things, I must attempt to fashion my life (will) in harmony with what I sense to be his will. Therefore, prayer is profoundly personal and must involve my whole person in the search for God's will. The very effort to discipline my thoughts, attitudes and behavior to this end becomes, for me, prayer in its fullest meaning. The words, time or place for an act of prayer must take secondary significance in relation to the invariable conscious need to seek the divine will in all that I strive to be and do. Thus, prayer for me is much like breathing. There can be no adequate words, or appropriate time, posture, or place that commands significance over a life of prayer. Rather the ingredients of reverence, sincerity, humility and faith, all emanating from the attitude of mind and heart, comprise the essence of the search for God's will, and the constancy of that search represents the meaning of prayer for me.

The act of prayer in a formal setting, such as a service of worship, either before or after a sermon, represents an effort to focus both mind and heart on the search for what may be God's will for his people through the proclamation of the Gospel. Likewise, intercessory prayer is of particular value in that the scope of conscious concern expands to include others with whom I may identify and empathize in a common search for the divine will and the resulting willingness to accept that will.

So much has been spoken and written about Dr. Martin Luther King, Jr. However, very little is said about the role of prayer in his life and ministry. The following passages from *Strength to Love* are, therefore, especially significant both for the content of the accounts and the power of prayer in the life of its author.

The idea that man expects God to do everything leads inevitably to a callous misuse of prayer. For if God does everything, man then asks him for anything, and God becomes little more than a "cosmic bellhop" who is summoned for every trivial need. Or God is considered so omnipotent and man so powerless that prayer is a substitute for work and intelligence. A man said to me, "I believe in integration, but I know it will not come until God wants it to come. You Negroes should stop protesting and start praying." I am certain we need to pray for God's help and guidance in this integration struggle, but we are gravely misled if we think the struggle will be won only by prayer. God, who gave us minds for thinking and bodies for working, would defeat his own purpose if he permitted us to obtain through prayer what may come through work and intelligence. Prayer is a marvelous and necessary supplement of our feeble efforts, but it is a dangerous substitute. When Moses strove to lead the Israelites to the Promised Land, God made it clear that he would not do for them what they could do for themselves. "And the Lord said unto Moses, Wherefore criest thou unto me? speak unto the children of Israel, that they go forward."

We must pray earnestly for peace, but we must also work vigorously for disarmament and the suspension of weapon testing. We must use our minds as rigorously to plan for peace as we have used them to plan for war. We must pray with unceasing passion for racial justice, but we

Prayer for Personal Devotions

must also use our minds to develop a programme, organize ourselves into mass nonviolent action, and employ every resource of our bodies and souls to bring an end to racial injustice. We must pray unrelentingly for economic justice, but we must also work diligently to bring into being those social changes that make for a better distribution of wealth within our nation and in the undeveloped countries of the world . . . .

Therefore we must never feel that God will, through some breath-taking miracle or a wave of the hand, cast evil out of the world. As long as we believe this we will pray unanswerable prayers and ask God to do things that he will never do. The belief that God will do everything for man is as untenable as the belief that man can do everything for himself. It, too, is based on a lack of faith. We must learn that to expect God to do everything while we do nothing is not faith, but superstition (pp. 131-132).

After a particularly strenuous day, I settled in bed at a late hour. My wife had already fallen asleep and I was about to doze off when the telephone rang. An angry voice said, "Listen, nigger, we've taken all we want from you. Before next week you'll be sorry you ever came to Montgomery." I hung up, but I could not sleep. It seemed that all of my fears had come down on me at once. I had reached the saturation point.

I got out of bed and began to walk the floor. Finally, I went to the kitchen and heated a pot of coffee. I was ready to give up. I tried to think of a way to move out of the picture without appearing to be a coward. In this state of exhaustion, when my courage had almost gone, I decided to take my problem to God. My head in my hands, I bowed over the kitchen table and prayed aloud. The words I spoke to God that midnight are still vivid in my memory. "I am here taking a stand for what I believe is right. But now I am afraid. The people are looking to me for leadership, and if I stand before them without strength and courage, they too will falter. I am at the end of my powers. I have nothing left. I've come to the point where I can't face it alone."

At that moment I experienced the presence of the Divine as I had never before experienced him. It seemed as though I could hear the quiet assurance of an inner voice, saying, "Stand up for righteousness, stand up for truth. God will be at your side forever." Almost at once my fears began to pass from me. My uncertainty disappeared. I was ready to face anything (p. 113).

In the light of Dr. King's testimony, this prayer by W. Maurice King in *Soul and Soil* takes on even more meaning. If we pray these words in the spirit of which King speaks, and thereby embody the action called faith, there might truly be a time of community instead of chaos.

Help us, Lord, to avoid the sin of racism—whether it be yellow, black, red, or white. Teach us to see a man as a person, a woman as a person, a child as a person. May we never become misguided and miss the freeway to truly abundant living because we refuse to listen to the directions that come from one whose culture, color, or class may be unlike our own. May we use the precious hours You give us to create means to purify the air we breathe, to cause the streams to sparkle again, so giving a new lease on life to fish and fowl and animal alike. May we use our lamps to light the way to brotherhood, to create the environment in which crime will become extinct, policemen will be seen as guides instead of guards, restraint will replace riots. Grant us Your help that we may one day enjoy community instead of chaos. *Amen.*

Perhaps the statements and prayers that follow will strike a responsive note in the readers own experience.

These are the words and prayers of lay persons as well as clergy. They address a variety of personal feelings and needs. But there is a common quality that gathers up the sense of "soul," that character of the black religious experience which is at one and the same time both unique and universal.

Prayer of Commitment

My dear loving Father in Heaven—how great You are. You are the Creator of all things and through You all things have been done, are being done, and can be done. Oh God—I praise Your wonderful name. Thank You gracious God for the many things that You have given me and I take for granted. Eyes to see the beauty of this world, ears to hear the precious Word, a voice to sing Your praises and to tell the good news of Your love, and Your sweet Holy Spirit that lives in me day to day. Help me not to complain about the earthly things I don't have, but to rejoice over all the things I do have and to share them with others.

O Lord, if you gave me what I deserved, I would be burning in hellfire right now for all the evil things I have done in my life and for the mistakes I've made recently. But through the sacrifice of Your only Son, You have redeemed me—Praise God—and blotted out my past, and now You can only see me as Your *will* would have me to be. O Lord, help me to see that *will*, to do that *will*. Help me to put my wants and desires behind me and only do what You want me to do, be what You want me to be, and say what You want me to say.

The deepest desire of my heart is to see You face to face in the land beyond the river, on the streets of gold, inside the pearly gates of Heaven—FOREVER. I ask nothing material of my life and to have the courage to walk in the path You have made for me with no fear of failing or being made fun of. I long to hear Your sweet voice say, "Well done, my good and faithful servant—enter into your reward that is in Heaven."

Thank you for your Son Jesus that was spit upon, whipped with a terrible whip, cursed at, and crucified on an old rugged cross for me. And in His wonderful sweet name, I ask these things and praise Your name.

Hallelujah! *Amen.*

By a child of the King

A Child's Prayer Poem

As I say my prayers at night,
I know that things will be all right.
Tomorrow will bring lots of Joy,
And happiness for each girl and boy.

Erica Hart

Prayer in the Life of a Young Adult

Prayer is something that is outstanding in a young person's life. Being a young adult is hard. For a while you feel like there's no one you can talk to and if you can find someone—they probably wouldn't understand. But after you stop and think, there is someone: God. Saying a prayer can't solve every problem but it can help you deal with it. Maybe just knowing that you have a friend wherever you go, who can be there whenever you want to talk is security. Prayer for some is the only way to survive an entire day.

Angie Rice

Prayer for Personal Devotions

Several years ago, a friend and I had planned to attend a weekend session of a conference about 250 miles away. In order to have more time there, she suggested that we fly. I had never flown before. I asked my parents what I should do. They told me that it was my decision to make. After some thought, I decided to fly. When I entered the plane and took my seat, I bowed my head and prayed. The flight there was a wonderful experience seeing the handiwork of God in the beauty of sky and earth. Returning, the flight was delayed for two hours because of a torrential rain storm. When we did board the plane, again, I bowed my head and prayed. I do not recall my exact words, but I prayed to God that whatever might happen I would be in His keeping. A feeling of peace and calmness seemed to come over me and I relaxed. The plane ride was very rough, not smooth as before, and many passengers became ill. We had been up much longer than flight time. My other two friends looked worriedly across at me and said, "Do you know that we are in a terrible storm and you don't even seem to be afraid?" I said to them, I prayed when I got into this plane that in either life or death I would be safe in God's care." *Prayer:* Dear God, thank you for helping me to know that it is not the length of prayer, but faith to believe that prayer will be answered. *Amen.*

Elmira Higgins

I am very concerned about the breaking down of the family structure, drug addiction among our youth, and unrest around the world. Prayer is needed for healing, both spiritual and physical. I hope this prayer for a better person, community, and world will make life more beautiful.

Father above, bless us with peace and harmony in our homes. Make them safe for rearing children. Take away stress, fear, and anger. Let them be safe harbors where love and caring abide. May they become institutions to make for a better society. *Amen.*

Josephine M. Moore

Prayer for Peace and Harmony in Our Home

Father above, who does bless us with peace and harmony, I come to Thee in this hour asking Thee to please bless and guide us. Guide me, especially, Lord, for Thou knowest all things and can lead me with love and prayer. Please do bless our home, Father. Let it become a home of peace and prayer. Help us to make our home life loving and happy. Help us to respond to Thy love by loving others in return. Help us to be patient one to another and to speak softly—and to put away our bitterness and wrath and anger. Help us to learn to live together here in the loving relationship of our Lord with all of Thy children here on earth.

O dear Father in Heaven, even as I am praying to Thee now for help and guidance, I know that Thou art sending the blessings I need. My heart is not troubled now nor afraid, for Thou comest to me as I pray to Thee in Thy Son's name. *Amen.*

Anonymous

I am happy
because You have accepted
me,
dear Lord.
Sometimes I do not know

what to do
with all my happiness.
I swim in Your grace
like a whale in the ocean.
The saying goes:
"An Ocean never dries up,"
but we know that Your grace also never fails.
Dear Lord,
Your grace is our happiness.
Hallelujah!

A young African in *Sing and Pray and Shout Hurray!* compiled by Roger Ortmayer

O God, help us live daily in the light of the glory of your victory in Jesus Christ, a victory over sin and death and all that destroys human life. Draw us by the power of that victory to live victoriously and confidently, even in the midst of trials and suffering, to know that you are faithful and that your victory is sure and certain. Through Jesus Christ our Lord. *Amen.*

Joseph Lincoln Allen

O God, Great and Creative Spirit, hear the cries of our heart and the longings within us for freedom and liberation. *Amen.*

Valerie E. Russell in *Liberation and Unity*

O God, give us a sense of awareness that thou art able to make us whole. Help us this day to embrace your gospel of liberation in order that we might know the freedom that only you can give. *Amen.*

Cecil W. Howard in *Liberation and Unity*

Grant, O God, that the transcending love of Christ bring new hope to those who suffer social injustice for what they believe and for who they are. *Amen.*

Eugene G. Turner in *Liberation and Unity*

O God of grace and mercy, lead the undecided to decisiveness. Lead the complacent to action. Lead the disappointed and discouraged to a closer walk with Thee. And most of all, Dear God, lead on those who feel they have totally apprehended Christ—from whereever they are. *Amen.*

Theodore A. Moore in *Liberation and Unity*

We pray for the day when the Black Church is contemporary, developmental, and ecumenical; and empowerment, liberation and community is the context in which all peoples live. We ask it in the name of Him who embodies all these petitions. *Amen.*

John Hurst Adams in *Liberation and Unity*

O God, our creator, you have given us so much, not least being the gift of life. Help us to constantly celebrate that which makes us unique. May we never again attempt to hide or disguise these traits. Guide us in the work to establish your Kingdom through actualization of all we were created to be. *Amen.*

Juanita Elizabeth Carroll in *Liberation and Unity*

Dear God, we thank you for your constant love and forgiving spirit. May each of us, as we acknowledge our sins, be receptive to you, not only in times of trouble but in moments of great joy. *Amen.*

Cornelius L. Henderson in *The Upper Room Disciplines 1983*

Increase our faith, O Lord. Make us bold as Abraham and all those who "died in faith, not having received what was promised, but having seen it and greeted it from afar." *Amen.*

Joseph B. Bethea in *The Upper Room Disciplines 1983*

Increase our faith, O Lord. Help us to find you in every experience we face so that each may be used for growth and your glory. *Amen.*

Joseph B. Bethea in *The Upper Room Disciplines 1983*

O God, we know we are not what we ought to be. We have failed to be the persons you intended for us to be. Nevertheless, remind us daily that we are called to be saints. In the name of Christ we pray. *Amen.*

Gilbert H. Caldwell in *The Upper Room Disciplines 1983*

O God, we ask that we may set our inhibitions aside and worship you freely with our whole being. *Amen.*

Gilbert H. Caldwell in *The Upper Room Disciplines 1983*

Heavenly Father, I come to you as your humble and thankful servant and child, for it is only through Your

Love, Mercy, Blessings and Kindness that I exist. Give me the wisdom please, Dear Lord, to use everything You have given me to follow the Glory of Your Name.

Thank you, Dear Jesus, for saving my soul, thank you for your Love. Thank you for giving me hope and faith. I pray that I may cleanse my heart and mind so that I may be in the Kingdom of God with You and my loved ones. I beg, Dear God, for your continued blessings and that I may stay in Your Grace and that Your Presence will be with me forever.

I pray that all of mankind will awaken and serve you, Dear Father, and they shall know that You are the Power and the Glory and the Master forever and ever.

Praise Your Holy Name, Dear God—I love You.

John W. Powell, Jr.

Recorded in *The Life Experience and Gospel Labors of the Rt. Rev. Richard Allen,* the contrasting experience of Richard Allen as a slave and as a worshiper in St. George's Church may help us grasp the powerful significance of prayer in the lives of blacks. Certainly the powerful prayers of Rev. Allen grew out of such experiences.

> My master was an unconverted man, and all the family, but he was what the world called a good master. He was more like a father to his slaves than anything else. He was a very tender, humane man. My mother and father lived with him for many years. He was brought into difficulty, not being able to pay for us, and mother having several children after he had bought us, he sold my mother and three children. My mother sought the Lord and found favor with him, and became a very pious woman. There were three children of us remained with our old master. . . .
>
> We frequently went to meeting on every other Thursday; but if we were likely to be backward with our crops

Prayer for Personal Devotions

we would refrain from going to meeting. When our master found we were making no provision to go to meeting, he would frequently ask us if it was not our meeting day, and if we were not going. We would frequently tell him: "No, sir, we would rather stay at home and get our work done." He would tell us: "Boys, I would rather you would go to your meeting; if I am not good myself, I would like to see you striving yourselves to be good." Our reply would be: "Thank you, sir, but we would rather stay and get our crops forward." So we always continued to keep our crops more forward than our neighbors, and we would attend public preaching once in two weeks, and class meeting once a week. At length, our master said he was convinced that religion made slaves better and not worse, and often boasted of his slaves for their honesty and industry. Some time after, I asked him if I might ask the preachers to come and preach at his house. He being old and infirm, my master and mistress cheerfully agreed for me to ask some of the Methodist preachers to come and preach at his house. . . .

A number of us usually attended St. George's church in Fourth Street; and when the colored people began to get numerous in attending the church, they moved us from the seats we usually sat on, and placed us around the wall, and so on Sabbath morning we went to the church and the sexton stood at the door, and told us to go in the gallery. He told us to go, and we would see where to sit. We expected to take the seats over the ones we formerly occupied below, not knowing any better. We took those seats. Meeting had begun, and they were nearly done singing, and just as we got to the seats, the elder said, "Let us pray." We had not been long upon our knees before I heard considerable scuffling and low talking. I raised my head up and saw one of the trustees, H____ M____, having hold of the Rev. Absalom Jones, pulling him up off of his knees, and saying, "You must get up—you must not kneel here." Mr. Jones replied, "Wait until prayer is over." Mr. H____ M____ said "No, you must get up now, or I will call for aid and force you away." Mr. Jones said, "Wait until prayer is over, and I will get up and trouble you no more." With that he beckoned to one of the other trustees, Mr. L____ S____ to come to his assistance. He came, and went to William White to pull him up. By this time prayer was over, and we all went out of the church in a body, and they were no more plagued with us in the church.

The three lengthy prayers of Richard Allen which follow capture the whole range of characteristics of prayer in the black tradition. They are virtually meditations in their own right. One could use them either for personal devotions or in public worship, especially as altar prayers. In developing one's own prayer, they are rich resources to draw upon. As recorded prayers of one of Christianity's great black representatives, they are a significant contribution worthy of including here.

Acts of Faith

I believe, O God, that Thou art an eternal, incomprehensible spirit, infinite in all perfections; who didst make all things out of nothing, and dost govern them all by thy wise providence.

Let me always adore Thee with profound humility, as my Sovereign Lord; and help me to love and praise thee with godlike affections and suitable devotion.

I believe that in the unity of the Godhead, there is a trinity of persons, that Thou art perfectly one and perfectly three; one essence and three persons. I believe, O blessed Jesus, that Thou art of one substance with the Father, the very and eternal God; that Thou didst take upon Thee our frail nature; that Thou didst truly suffer, and wert crucified, dead and buried, to reconcile us to thy Father and to be a sacrifice for sin.

I believe, that according to the types and prophecies, which went before, of Thee, and according to Thy own

Prayer for Personal Devotions

infallible prediction, Thou didst by Thy own power rise from the dead and the third day, that Thou didst ascend into Heaven, that there Thou sittest on Thy throne of glory adored by angels and interceding for sinners.

I believe, that Thou hast instituted and ordained holy mysteries, as pledges of Thy love, and for a continual commemoration of Thy death; that Thou hast not only given Thyself to die for me, but to be my spiritual food and sustenance in that holy sacrament to my great and endless comfort. O, may I frequently approach Thy altar with humility and devotion, and work in me all those holy and heavenly affections, which become the remembrance of a crucified Saviour.

I believe, O Lord, that Thou hast not abandoned me to the dim light of my own reason to conduct me to happiness, but that Thou hast revealed in the Holy Scriptures whatever is necessary for me to believe and practice, in order to my eternal salvation.

Oh, how noble and excellent are the precepts; how sublime and enlightening the truth; how persuasive and strong the motives; how powerful the assistance of Thy holy religion, in which Thou hast instructed me; my delight shall be in Thy statutes, and I will not forget Thy word.

I believe it is my greatest honor and happiness to be thy disciple; how miserable and blind are those that live without God in the world, who despise the light of Thy holy faith. Make me to part with all the enjoyments of life; nay, even life itself, rather than forfeit this jewel of great price. Blessed are the sufferings which are endured, happy is the death which is undergone for heavenly and immortal truth! I believe that Thou hast prepared for those that love Thee, everlasting mansions of glory; if I believe Thee, O, eternal happiness. Why does anything appear difficult that leads to Thee? Why should I not willingly resist unto blood to obtain Thee? Why do the vain and empty employments of life take such vast hold of us? O, perishing time! Why dost Thou thus bewitch and deceive me? O, blessed eternity! When shalt Thou be my portion forever?

Acts of Hope

O, my God! in all my dangers, temporal and spiritual, I will hope in thee who art Almighty power, and therefore able to relieve me; who art infinite goodness, and therefore ready and willing to assist me.

O, precious blood of my dear Redeemer! O, gaping wounds of my crucified Saviour! Who can contemplate the sufferings of God incarnate, and not raise his hope, and not put his trust in Him? What, though my body be crumpled into dust, and that dust blown over the face of the earth, yet I undoubtedly know my Redeemer lives, and shall raise me up at the last day; whether I am comforted or left desolate; whether I enjoy peace or am afflicted with temptations; whether I am healthful or sickly, succored or abandoned by the good things of this life, I will always hope in thee, O, my chiefest, infinite good.

Although the fig-tree shall not blossom, neither shall fruit be in the vines; although the labor of the olive shall fail, and the fields yield no meat; although the flock shall be cut off from the fold, and there shall be no herd in the stalls, yet I will rejoice in the Lord, I will joy in the God of my salvation.

What, though I mourn and am afflicted here, and sigh under the miseries of this world for a time, I am sure that my tears shall one day be turned into joy, and that joy none shall take from me. Whoever hopes for the great things in this world, takes pains to attain them; how can my hopes of everlasting life be well grounded, if I do not strive and labor for that eternal inheritance? I will never refuse the meanest labors, while I look to receive such glorious wages; I will never repine at any temporal loss, while I expect to gain such eternal rewards. Blessed hope! Be thou my chief delight in life, and then I shall be steadfast and immovable, always abounding in the work of the Lord; be thou my comfort and support at the hour of death, and then I shall contentedly leave this world, as a captive that is released from his imprisonment.

Acts of Love

O, infinite amiableness! When shall I love thee without bounds? without coldness or interruption, which, alas! so often seize me here below? Let me never suffer any creature to be Thy rival, or to share my heart with Thee; let me have no other God, no other love, but only Thee.

Whoever loves, desires to please the beloved object; and according to the degree of love is the greatness of desire; make me, O God! diligent and earnest in pleasing Thee; let me cheerfully discharge the most painful and costly duties; and forsake friends, riches, ease and life itself, rather than disobey Thee.

Whoever loves, desires the welfare and happiness of the beloved object; but Thou, O dear Jesus, can'st receive no addition from my imperfect services; what shall I do to express my affection towards Thee? I will relieve the necessities of my poor brethren, who are members of Thy body; for he that loveth not his brother whom he has seen, how can he love God whom he hath not seen?

O, crucified Jesus! in whom I live, and without whom I die; mortify in me all sensual desires; inflame my heart with Thy holy love, that I may no longer esteem the vanities of this world, but place my affections entirely on Thee.

Let my last breath, when my soul shall leave my body,

breathe forth love to Thee, my God; I entered into life without acknowledging Thee, let me therefore finish it in loving Thee; O let the last act of life be love, remembering that God is love.

Richard Allen in *The Life Experience and Gospel Labors of the Rt. Rev. Richard Allen*

No collection of prayers out of the Black tradition would be complete without contributions from Dr. Howard Thurman. The concluding prayer in this section was included in a commemorative issue of *Toward Wholeness, The Journal of Ministries to Blacks in Higher Education* (Spring 1983).

The Listening Ear

Give me the listening ear. I seek this day the ear that will not shrink from the word that corrects and admonishes—the word that holds up before me the image of myself that causes me to pause and reconsider—the word that challenges me to deeper consecration and higher resolve—the word that lays bare needs that make my own days uneasy, that seizes upon every good decent impulse of my nature, channeling it into paths of healing in the lives of others.

Give me the listening ear. I seek this day the disciplined mind, the disciplined heart, the disciplined life that makes my ear the focus of attention through which I may become mindful of expressions of life foreign to my own. I seek the stimulation that lifts me out of old ruts and established habits which keep me conscious of my self, my needs, my personal interests.

Give me this day—the eye that is willing to see the meaning of the ordinary, the familiar, the commonplace—the eye that is willing to see my own faults for what they are—the eye that is willing to see the likable qualities in those I may not like—the mistake in what I thought was correct—the strength in what I had labeled as weakness. Give me the eye that is willing to see that Thou hast not left Thyself without a witness in every living thing. Thus to walk with reverence and sensitiveness through all the days of my life.

Give me the listening ear
The eye that is willing to see.

Howard Thurman

4
PRAYER IN BLACK LITERATURE

Betty L. Hart

Black life is a drama. Black people understand it as drama. They act out life in a world in which they are called upon to play many roles—cool, striving, assimilative, spiritual people. The stage for this drama is set by the variety of experiences which black people must encounter in shifting in and out of various worlds—work worlds, home worlds, church worlds.

In this metaphor of black life as drama, prayer is the black person's soliloquy before the audience of God. In prayer, we lower our masks to reveal our native selves, expressing our weakness and our humility and baring our souls for judgment.

Prayer is a creative, personal expression in which we seek affirmation of our purpose and significance in this world. Prayer, as it occurs in literature, often serves as the device for expressing the profound truths of our moral character. In black literature, prayer expresses not only life's profound truths, but it also interprets the intensity of life's realities. Religion and prayer are very much a part of the black experience. It is and always will be for black people a constant source of comfort and strength to call upon God in time of need, joy, and praise. In literature, life's artistic mirror, the black person's faith and resource to God is no less significant.

In most literary fiction, prayer is incidental to the lives of the characters; in black literature, it is indigenous to the experience of its characters and hence significant in its value as a mode for focusing events and persons in perspective to the plot and overall theme of the work. In prayer, black people express their perceptions of and reactions to life in their worlds. They tell God about their troubles, their needs, their anger. They ask God to protect them, comfort them, forgive them, bless them, and most of all give them strength and understanding to cope with life in a hostile, threatening world. Often in these literary prayers, the black speakers acknowledge their inferiority to God, yielding to a resignation to their plight and a desire to leave their problems to God. God is comforter, master, and father.

Just as the character of religion and life in black culture has changed over the years, so has the nature and attitude of blacks toward those things changed in prayers in contemporary black literature. The early themes of black prayers in literature convey the message of people in bondage, struggling to survive and forever believing in God's ability to deliver them from sorrow and suffering. There is a resignation to the trials of life and a faith in a better hereafter. Over the years, that faith and hope have remained, but the theme has taken on additional messages to God: impatience and anger for the exclusivity of their plight, despair over the endless conditions of poverty, and doubt that God truly intends to relieve them in this life.

Another feature of black prayer which has changed is the tone and style of the language. The speakers of literary black prayers written prior to the racially tense 1960s period have a tone of humility, submission, and innocent faith. But by the 1960s, resentment and weariness wore the spiritual conscience of black artists thin. Typical of the angry messages of prayers in black literature is Charles Anderson's poem, "Prayer to the White Man's God," in which Anderson expresses the futility of prayer to a God who, indifferent to the poet's voice, tells Anderson to "go 'way boy." This is the white God whose repertoire of concerns does not take account of the injustices and suffering endured by the black voices lifted in prayer. The poet's anger speaks out as he acknowledges the existence of Jesus: "Cause he spit in my eye."

The prevailing tone of black literature of the late 1960s and early 1970s is angry, distrusting, and disillusioned. It speaks for a people who, perhaps at this point, are tired of "holding on" for those promises deep rooted in our faith—promises of no pain, no suffering, a better life, a land where "milk and honey flow." There is an impatience evident in this poetry. Clarence Reed in his poem, "In a Harlem Store Front Church," decries the "rhapsodic" seduction of the black race by its religious rituals. Instead Reed finds the source of strength, hope, and faith, not in God or worship, but in the shouting sisters themselves: "There is no more to God than you."

Black prayer of the latter twentieth century demonstrates the need for tangible evidence of God's presence and power in black lives. The language is direct and belligerent. Anderson's diction is colloquial: "Lord, what's the delay?" There is this tendency in contemporary black poetry to regard traditional values and cultural attitudes with some irreverence. Modern black poets must detach themselves by bitterness in order to clear the anger and frustration from their souls. Instead of begging the Lord for some attention, modern poets demand an audience with God and further demand justification for God's seeming indifference to their prior prayers.

W. E. B. Dubois' prose prayer from *Darkwater*, "A

Littany at Atlanta, done at Atlanta, in the Day of Death, 1906," ponders the existence of God as well. Yet the poem positively asserts the presence and changelessness of God:

> Wherefore do we pray? Is not the God of the fathers dead? Have not seers seen in Heaven's halls Thine hearsed and lifeless form stark amidst the black and rolling smoke of sin, where all along bow bitter forms of endless dead? . . . Thou art still the God of our black fathers, and in Thy soul's soul sit some soft darkenings of the evening, some shadowings of the velvet night.

Here the author combines the cadence of biblical language with the intensity of his commanding message. Whereas Dubois' God may seem dead, the writer at least maintains a faith that God will ultimately bring justice to the suffering and injustice endured by the black race. Likewise, other early black writers have this faith in God's ultimate deliverance of the race. Paul Laurence Dunbar's poetry, in particular, demonstrates an unshakeable faith in God as deliverer. From this faith, Dunbar believes the race may draw its strength to endure the present times in hope of a better tomorrow. Dunbar's poetry represents a dramatic contrast to modern poems in both language and theme. His poem, "Resignation," uses conventional biblical diction and poetic form. The tone of humility prevails.

> Long had I grieved at what I deemed abuse;
>   But now I am as grain within the mill.
> If so be thou must crush me for thy use,
>   Grind on O potent God, and do thy will!

The following Paul Dunbar poems are also exemplary of the traditional tone of prayerful humility:

A Prayer

O Lord, the hard-won miles
  Have worn my stumbling feet:
Oh, soothe me with thy smiles,
  And make my life complete.

The thorns were thick and keen
  Where'er I trembling trod;
The way was long between
  My wounded feet and God.

Where healing waters flow
  Do thou my footsteps lead.
My heart is aching so;
  Thy gracious balm I need.

A Hymn

Lead gently, Lord, and slow,
  For oh, my steps are weak,
And ever as I go,
  Some soothing sentence speak;
That I may turn my face
  Through doubt's obscurity
Toward thine abiding place,
  E'en tho' I cannot see.

For lo, the way is dark;
  Through mist and cloud I grope,
Save for that fitful spark,
  The little flame of hope.

Lead gently, Lord, and slow,
  For fear that I may fail;
I know not where to go
  Unless I hear thy call.

> My fainting soul doth yearn
> For thy green hills afar;
> So let thy mercy burn—
> My greater, guiding star!

The following two poems are similar to Dunbar's. In both poems, the speakers request that they be more Christlike in their dealings with others. In the first prayer, the speaker asks for love, compassion, forgiveness, and a better regard for humanity. In the second prayer, the speaker, like Dunbar in "Resignation," submits himself to God's will.

My Prayer

> Oh, Give me, Lord, Thy love for souls
> For lost and wandering sheep,
> That I may see the multitudes
> And weep as Thou didst weep.
> Help me to see the tragic plight
> Of souls far off in sin;
> Help me to love and pray and
> To bring the wandering in.

My Prayer

> O Fire of Life, O Flame Divine,
> Make Thine abode in me;
> Burn in my heart, burn evermore,
> Till I shine out for Thee.

J. Solomon Benn, III in *Preaching from the Bible*

Margaret Walker's prose poem celebrates the faith that keeps the hope of the black race moving forward. She touches upon the strengths and values of black culture that have sustained her people through the hard times and the hopeful years. It takes the form of prayer in her praise of black people and her request that God include them as part of "a new earth."

For My People

For my people everywhere singing their slave songs repeatedly:
    Their dirges and their ditties and their blues and jubilees, . . .
For my people lending their strength to the years, . . . washing ironing cooking scrubbing sewing mending hoeing plowing digging planting pruning patching . . .
For the . . . years we went to school to learn . . . when we discovered we were black and poor and small and different and nobody cared and nobody wondered and nobody understood;
For the boys and girls who grew in spite of these things to be man and woman, to laugh and dance and sing and play, . . . to marry their playmates bear children and then die of consumption and anemia and lynching; . . .
For my people standing staring . . . trying to fashion a world that will hold all the people, all the faces, all the adams and eves and their countless generations;
Let a new earth rise. Let another world be born . . . Let a second generation full of courage issue forth; let a people loving freedom come to growth . . . Let the martial songs be written, let the dirges disappear. Let a race of people now rise and take control.

Margaret Walker in *Drum Majors for Justice*

The stylistic range of language and tone in black prayers is varied and runs from traditional dialect in prayers like Dunbar's prayer poems and the unaffected simplicity of Owen Dodson's "Black Mother Praying" to the stark, and sometimes profane, diction of contemporary authors. Language range, that is facility with language, is an important element in black life. One's ability to use language creatively and in many contexts has a direct bearing on one's ability to survive and cope with the many obstacles in black life. And this holds true for any time in the history of black people. Thus, whether it is humility or anger, each poet or writer for the black experience is using the ultimate tool to give appropriate expression to the particular cultural orientation of the race to its God. The theme is consistent: deliverance, strength to endure, and justice. As prayer and religion are a large part of both black culture and black art, its usefulness as a vehicle for expression in literature is significant.

One particular feature of prayer in black life is its spontaneity as an oral form of discourse. As the speakers compose their prayers, they are shaping the raw data of their feelings into logical, natural discourse. This discourse requires the speakers to edit—organize and synthesize—their ideas and observations prior to expression. But the nature of black oral discourse has interpretation beyond the conventions of standard American English, for the oral tradition in black culture sees language more in terms of its creative potential than its functional power.

Sara Webster Fabio, in her essay, "Who Speaks Negro? What is Black?" in *Negro Digest* (Sept./Oct. 1968), describes the expressive attributes of black language:

> Black language is direct, creative, intelligent communication . . . (it) places premium on imagistic renderings and concretizations of abstractions, poetic usages . . . , idiosyncracies—those individualized stylistic nuances (such as violation of structured syntax)—which nevertheless hit "home" and evoke truth; it is an idiom of integrated insight, a knowledge emanating from a juxtaposition of feeling and fact.

Typical of this expressive character of black language is Owen Dodson's poem, "Black Mother Praying." This poignant commentary on the duality of black existence is poetic in its use of imagery, analogy, and poetic diction. The tone is personal and tactful. Here a mother converses with God in earnest, simple language, deploring the irony of blacks who must fight for their country abroad but who must fight against their country at home. As many black authors do in dealing with the theme of suffering and injustice, Dodson wisely chooses the archetypal figure of the black mother, who in addition to the usual, universal maternal sacrifices, must suffer the sorrow of seeing her children grow up in a world of cruel lies.

In this prayer, which takes the form of an informal conversation the mother reports to God the status of black life in America. She begins by thanking God for his comfort and assurance, "You been a tenderness to me . . . You been a pilla to my soul." And then she speaks her "peace", plainly and directly: "I'm gonna say my say real quick and simple." She tells the Lord of the sacrifice of her sons to this terrible war, a sacrifice not unlike God's sacrifice of his only Son. But she cannot reconcile her sacrifice of sons in a war which supposedly wants freedom for a country which denies freedom at home for her sons: "Freedom is writ big, and crossed out."

The hypocrisy of this lie is evident in the beatings, "the blood on the darkness," the fights, the burnings, and the lynchings. She asks, "What has we done?" Yet, despite her inability to comprehend the justice of this hate, she maintains her faith that God will bring justice to this land, to "plant Your Son's goodness in this land." She prays that God will bring deliverance to the beaten bodies and spirits of her people; otherwise, she would rather "let them die in the desert drinkin sand" than have them suffer in vain. After a graphic account of specific cruelties—a lynching, a rape, and the senseless beating of a black child, she begs the Lord, "How can I pray again?" The reference then is clearly to the correspondence of this cruelty to that suffered by Jesus: "Every time they strike us, they strikin Your Son." She will not give up until she and her sons realize their rightful freedom and peace and "people not afraid again." She asks God to "let us all see the golden wheat together." Her faith and hope that God will be the instrument of justice and deliverance provides her comfort and sustaining grace to accept her sacrifice of sons in war.

The role of prayer in black life goes beyond sustaining grace. In the following prose selections, the authors use prayer to address some of the other facets of black life. Both authors, John Oliver Killens and James Baldwin, adapt the tone and voice of the prayers to the personalities of the characters. Each writer is indicative of a different culture of black people—Killen's rural gathering and Baldwin's urban store front gathering.

John O. Killens' novel, *Youngblood,* is set in a sleepy, little Georgia mill town in the mid-1930s. The black community of Crossroads has planned its annual Jubilee Day program, an affair sanctioned by the white citizenry and providing the occasion for the "coloreds" to do a little singing and celebrating. Much to the chagrin of Ben Blake, school principal and appointed white overseer of the event, the program departs from tradition and highlights the historical and cultural significance of each of the Negro spirituals presented on the program. The audience, though deserted by most whites, gives a resounding "amen" of approval, but there is concern that the "militant" content of the program may have offended and angered the former white patrons of Jubilee Day. Prior to dismissal, the remaining audience is led in prayer by Reverend Ledbetter who comes forward with raised arms. Every head is bowed, including most of the white folks.

We thank you, O Heavenly Father, for this great gathering here tonight of black and white citizens, children of the Heavenly King. We hope that all of them have been caught up by the spirit of Negro spirituals, the spirit of peace on earth, good will to all men no matter their nationality or religion. We are humbly proud, Dear Father, of our spirituals, for they are some of the most glorious songs ever sung in the name of your Son, Jesus. But we want the world to know, O Merciful Father, that we, your black sons and daughters, haven't sung any songs like we're going to sing them one of these days—In that Great-Getting-Up-Morning, when we all cross over the River of Jordan, when all men on earth will be truly brothers in the sight of God and man, O Lord. We're going to sing a song we never sang before—We're going to sing like nobody ever sang before.

From *Youngblood* by John Oliver Killens

James Baldwin's setting for "Florence's Prayer" is an urban storefront church at that climactic point in the service which calls upon the lost souls to claim their salvation at the altar. Here, Florence in her desperate need for God's help and mercy, calls upon her memories of her mother praying. These memories overcome Florence's inadequacy and enable her prayers to rise eloquently to the occasion of her salvation.

Florence's Prayer

Kneeling as she had not knelt for many years, and in this company before the altar, she gained again from the song the meaning it had held for her mother, and gained a new meaning for herself. As a child, the song had made her see a woman, dressed in black, standing in infinite mists alone, waiting for the form of the Son of God to lead her through that white fire. This woman now returned to her, more desolate; it was herself, not knowing where to put her foot; she waited, trembling, for the mists to be parted that she might walk in peace. That long road, her life, which she had followed for sixty groaning years, had led her at last to her mother's starting-place, the altar of the Lord. For her feet stood on the edge of that river which her mother, rejoicing, had crossed over. And would the Lord now reach out His hand to Florence and heal and save? But, going down before the scarlet cloth at the foot of the golden cross, it came to her that she had forgotten how to pray.

Her mother had taught her that the way to pray was to forget everything and everyone but Jesus; to pour out the heart, like water from a bucket, all evil thoughts, all thoughts of self, all malice for one's enemies; to come boldly, and yet more humbly than a little child, before the Giver of all good things.

"Dear Father"—it was her mother praying—"we come before You on our knees this evening to ask You to watch over us and hold back the hand of the destroying angel. Lord, sprinkle the doorpost of this house with the blood of the Lamb to keep all the wicked men away. Lord, we praying for every mother's son and daughter everywhere in the world but we want You to take special care of this girl here tonight, Lord, and don't let no evil come nigh her. We know you's able to do it, Lord, in Jesus' name, Amen."

Her mother, dressed in the long, shapeless, colorless dress that she wore every day but Sunday, when she wore white, and with her head tied up in a scarlet cloth, knelt in the center of the room, her hands hanging loosely folded before her, her black face lifted, her eyes shut. The weak, unsteady light placed shadows under her mouth and in the sockets of her eyes, making the face impersonal with majesty, like the face of a prophetess, or like a mask. Silence filled the room after her "Amen" . . .

From *Go Tell It on the Mountain* by James Baldwin

The problem in discussing prayer in literature is the problem of formulating and justifying an equation in which we acknowledge that prayer for black people *is* conversation with God and that perhaps black people have been so creative in prayer because, for them, it has been one of the few truly democratic social forms which they have ever known—any and everyone is allowed equal access to and redress from the higher authority. In its creative form, prayer becomes a mode for unrestrained expression of self, both in the beautiful and ugly interpretations of one's environment.

It is hard to separate the idea and form of prayer from the messages of early spirituals, and even in contemporary black gospel music, the personal praises of and testimonies to God are not individually distinguishable as prayer and nonprayer. Perhaps it is that direct access to God through prayer that makes most expressive interpretations of a black person's religion prayerful by nature. Very little in the way of creative expression to God by a black person can *not* be prayer. Any writer who attempts to interpret the black experience through literature or song must surely know the usefulness of prayer as a creative resource. The omniscient voice that trespasses the mind and soul of a character can be established by using prayer. Consequently, prayer is a device for revealing the private spiritual personalities of black characters.

5

PRAYER IN SONG

Charlotte A. Meade

Music is not an addendum to the black worship experience, whether that experience be corporate or private. Music is basic. To borrow words from Dr. William B. McClain, "Singing is as close to worship as breathing is to life." The old African dictum that "the Spirit will not descend without a song" is deeply incorporated into Afro-Christian worship.

In the black church tradition, devotions are usually led by a deacon and precede the ascent of the pastor to the pulpit. Song testimonies, the Word, and fervent prayer are the ingredients needed to prepare our hearts and minds to come like "empty pitchers before a full fountain," whetting our thirst for the living water in the fountain of worship. A cappella singing, often raised as a testimony, becomes the accompaniment for prayer. Song and the spoken word blend into a composite praise offering to God.

Music often sets the tone for prayer; it evokes the prayer, cushions the prayer, ignites the prayer, fuels the prayer like kindling to a smoldering fire, and when the prayer comes to its close, music concludes the prayer, moving us less abruptly from the high place of a personal talk with God to the reality of our earthly station.

Often music *is* the prayer: "Precious Lord, take my hand." "Jesus, won't you come by here?" LeRoi Jones in *Blues People* traces, through the slave "citizen's" music, the path a slave took to citizenship. The African was taken from an intensely religious culture. Religion was a daily, minute-to-minute concern, not a once-a-week revelation. From the a cappella work songs, to the shout songs, to the spirituals, to the "borrowed" songs, to the blues, to the gospel songs, LeRoi Jones suggests that music is the result of thought, largely conditioned by reference to those life experiences—a reference that becomes very personal. In these songs which offer such spontaneous, personal interpretations, music is the prayerful expression of an individual's life experience. Music is thought perfected at its most empirical attitude or stance. How great must be the perfection of prayer thoughts set to music, for how perfect is the reference of that lyric.

The songs which wend their way into subconscious memory become the backdrop for private and corporate worship. The prayer songs do not get their significance from who wrote the songs. Their power comes from the immediate relevance of the song's message. Black people can find the beat and melody to help transport a lyric to the realms of their experiences. Many lyrics shared in this section were not written by black writers, for the black experience has not excluded that which speaks truth, wherever it was found.

Dear Jesus, I Love You

Dear Jesus, I Love You.
Dear, Jesus, I love You,
You're a friend of mine.

You supply my every need.
My hungry soul You feed.
I'm aware You are my source
From which all blessings flow,
And with this thought in mind
I know just where to go.

"Dear Jesus, I Love You" by Walter Hawkins. © Copyright 1976 by Libris Music BMI. All rights reserved. International copyright secured. used by Special Permission.

Close to Thee

Thou my everlasting portion,
More than friend or life to me,
All along my pilgrim journey,
Savior, let me walk with Thee.
Not for ease or worldly pleasure,
Nor for fame my prayer shall be;
Gladly will I toil and suffer,
Only let me walk with Thee.
Lead me through the vale of shadows,
Bear me o'er life's fitful sea;
Then the gate of life eternal
May I enter, Lord, with Thee.
Close to Thee, Close to Thee,
Close to Thee, Close to Thee,
All along my pilgrim journey,
Savior, let me walk with Thee.

Fannie J. Crosby

Father, I Stretch My Hands To Thee

Father, I stretch my hands to Thee,
No other help I know;
If Thou withdraw Thyself from me,
Ah! whither shall I go?

Prayer In The Black Tradition

What did Thine only Son endure,
Before I drew my breath!
What pain, what labor to secure
My soul from endless death!
Surely Thou canst not let me die,
O speak and I shall live;
And here I will unwearied lie,
Till Thou Thy spirit give.
Author of faith! to Thee I lift
My weary, longing eyes;
O let me now receive that gift!
My soul without it dies.

Charles Wesley

Jesus, Keep Me Near The Cross

Jesus, keep me near the cross;
There's a precious fountain,
Free to all, a healing stream,
Flows from Calvary's mountain.
Near the cross! O Lamb of God,
Bring its scenes before me;
Help me walk from day to day
With its shadows o'er me.
In the cross, in the cross,
Be my glory ever,
Till my raptured soul shall find
Rest beyond the river.

Fanny J. Crosby from *Songs of Zion* no. 19. Verses 1, 3, and the refrain.

Lift Every Voice and Sing

Verse 3:
God of our weary years,
God of our silent tears,

Thou who hast brought us thus far on the way;
Thou who hast by thy might,
Led us into the light,
Keep us forever in the path, we pray.
Lest our feet stray from the places, our God,
    where we met Thee,
Lest our hearts, drunk with the wine of the
    world, we forget Thee;
Shadowed beneath Thy hand,
May we forever stand,
True to our God,
True to our native land.

"Lift Every Voice and Sing" (James Weldon Johnson, J. Rosamond Johnson) © Copyright: Edward B. Marks Music Company. Used by permission. *Songs of Zion* no. 32.

Lead Me to Calvary

King of my life I crown Thee now—
Thine shall the glory be;
Lest I forget Thy thorn-crowned brow,
Lead me to Calvary.
Show me the tomb where Thou wast laid,
Tenderly mourned and wept;
Angels in robes of light arrayed
Guarded Thee whilst Thou slept.
Let me, like Mary, through the gloom,
Come with a gift to Thee;
Show to me now the empty tomb—
Lead me to Calvary.
May I be willing, Lord, to bear
Daily my cross for Thee;
Even Thy cup of grief to share—
Thou hast borne all for me.
Lest I forget Gethsemane,
Lest I forget Thine agony,

Lest I forget Thy love for me,
Lead me to Calvary.

Jennie Evelyn Hussey

Just a Closer Walk With Thee

Just a closer walk with Thee;
Grant it, Jesus, if you please,
Daily walking close with Thee,
Let it be, dear Lord, let it be.
I am weak but Thou art strong,
Jesus, keep me from all wrong,
I'll be satisfied as long,
As I walk, Let me walk close with Thee.
Through this world of toils and snares,
If I falter, Lord, who cares?
Who with me my burdens shares?
None but Thee, dear Lord, none but Thee.
When my feeble life is o'er,
Time for me won't be no more,
Guide me gently, safely o'er,
To Thy kingdom shore, to Thy shore.

(Traditional)

Lord, Don't Move The Mountain

Lord, don't move the mountain,
But give me strength to climb it.
Please don't move that stumbling block,
But lead me, Lord, around it.
The way may not be easy.
You didn't say that it will be;
For when our tribulations get too light,
We tend to stray from Thee.

Now when my enemies would slay me,
And these things they will try to do;
Oh Lord, don't touch him, but within his heart,
Make him give his heart to You.
Our cares we bring unto You,
You told us that we could;
For You help those who try to help themselves
And I believe we should.

Doris Akers
© Copyright 1958 Manna Music, Inc. 2111 Kenmere Ave., Burbank, CA 91504, International copyright secured. All rights reserved. Used by permission.

Some Day

Beams of heaven, as I go,
Through this wilderness below,
Guide my feet in peaceful ways,
Turn my midnights into days;
When in the darkness I would grope,
Faith always sees a star of hope,
And soon from all life's grief and danger,
I shall be free some day.

Refrain: I do not know how long 'twill be,
Nor what the future holds for me,
But this I know, if Jesus leads me,
I shall get home some day.

Oftentimes my sky is clear,
Joy abounds without a tear,
Though a day so bright begun,
Clouds may hide tomorrow's sun.
There'll be a day that's always bright,
A day that never yields to night,
And in its light the streets of glory
I shall behold some day.

Prayer In The Black Tradition

Refrain

Harder yet may be the fight,
Right may often yield to might,
Wickedness awhile may reign,
Satan's cause may seem to gain;
There is a God that rules above,
With hand of pow'r and heart of love,
If I am right, He'll fight my battle,
I shall have peace some day.

Refrain

Burdens now may crush me down,
Disappointments all around,
Troubles speak in mournful sigh,
Sorrow through a tear-stained eye;
There is a world where pleasure reigns,
No mourning soul shall roam its plains,
And to that land of peace and glory
I want to go some day.

Refrain

Lord, Help Me To Hold Out

Lord, help me to hold out,
Lord, help me to hold out,
Lord, help me to hold out
Until my change comes.
My way may not be easy
You did not say that it would be.
But if it gets dark,
I can't see my way,
You told me to put my trust in Thee,
That's why I'm asking You.
Lord, help me to hold out,
Until my change comes.

I believe I can hold out,
Until my change comes.

James Cleveland

Stand by Me

When the storms of life are raging,
Stand by me;
When the storms of life are raging,
Stand by me.
When the world is tossing me,
Like a ship upon the sea;
Thou who rulest wind and water,
Stand by me.

In the midst of tribulation,
Stand by me;
In the midst of tribulation,
Stand by me.
When the hosts of hell assail,
And my strength begins to fail,
Thou who never lost a battle,
Stand by me.

In the midst of faults and failures,
Stand by me;
In the midst of faults and failures,
Stand by me.
When I do the best I can,
And my friends misunderstand,
Thou who knowest all about me,
Stand by me.

In the midst of persecution,
Stand by me;
In the midst of persecution,

Stand by me.
When my foes in battle array
Undertake to stop my way,
Thou who saved Paul and Silas,
Stand by me.

When I'm growing old and feeble,
Stand by me;
When I'm growing old and feeble,
Stand by me.
When my life becomes a brden,
And I'm nearing chilly Jordan,
O Thou "Lily of the Valley,"
Stand by me.

Charles A. Tindley

Revive Us Again

We praise Thee, O God, for the Son of Thy love,
For Jesus who died and is now gone above.
We praise Thee, O God, for Thy spirit of light,
Who has shown us our Savior and banished our night.
All glory and praise to the Lamb that was slain,
Who has taken our sins and has cleansed every stain.
Revive us again—fill each heart with Thy love;
May each soul be rekindled with fire from above.
Hallelujah, Thine the glory! Hallelujah, amen!
Hallelujah, Thine the Glory! Revive us again.

William P. Mackay

I Need Thee Every Hour

I need thee every hour, most gracious Lord;
No tender voice like thine can peace afford.
I need thee every hour; stay thou near by;

Temptations lose their power when thou art nigh.
I need thee every hour, in joy or pain;
Come quickly and abide, or life is vain.
I need thee every hour; teach me thy will;
And thy rich promises in me fulfill.
I need thee, O I need thee,
Every hour I need thee;
O bless me now, my Savior,
I come to thee!

Annie S. Hawks

A CONCLUDING PERSONAL SHARING

I thank God for the gift of song. It's not the only gift God has given me, and I am not the only one to whom this gift has been given. We may not share equally in our talent of rendering the song, but all can share deeply in the benefits of its healing ministry.

Lyrics, like scriptures, take on new dimensions of interpretation in the light of additional experiences. Songs that in my youth seemed "old folksy" and "draggy" or "sad" and "without a beat," now, in my middle age, are solid, sustaining, a firm foundation. The words to songs which I memorized in my youth, not because I was aware of their profundity but due to the frequency with which they were sung, now come back as a balm, yea, even a shield against afflictions and a staff for sure footing on those stumbling blocks.

Music is an integral part of my waking hours. It wends its way into my friendly banterings and those deep, soul-searching times with my Savior and best friend. Charles Allen in *The Touch of the Master's Hand* suggests that no person really prays until he has a need that his own resources are insufficient to meet. Such times are the "soul-searching" times.

The music and lyrics that permeate my very soul elude color or racial barriers. The lyrics strike a familiar experiential chord, and the song becomes my song. I claim it whether listening to it, singing it, teaching it, or praying it.

Prayer for me takes a formal posture from time to time, but most often it is a walking and talking with my best friend. Sometimes with questions like: Why? Why not? How long? When? Who? But most times in praise and thanksgiving and *always* in the faith and knowledge that I'm not alone: "He promised never to leave me, never to leave me alone."

I've had some times when I could not sing; when the emptiness within engulfed my voice; when the joy of the Lord seemed a memory of the yesterday, a hope for the tomorrow, but a stranger to that day. In those times, when I could not sing, God gave me songs . . . a literal feeding of spiritual food that I could think to God, play on the piano to God, and later read to God as my personal prayers, until God and I could renew my strength, restore my joy, and resume "normal" communication.

A very close friend was in physical danger, living in fear for her own well-being and for the well-being of those whom she loved. In praying for their protection and for deliverance from fear, these words from "How Firm a Foundation" came to me as vividly as if I had penned them myself:

> Fear not, I am with thee; O be not dismayed,
> For I am thy God, and will still give thee aid;
> I'll strengthen thee, help thee, and cause thee to stand,
> Upheld by my righteous, omnipotent hand.
> The soul that on Jesus still leans for repose,
> I will not, I will not desert to his foes;
> That soul, though all hell should endeavor to shake,
> I'll never, no, never, no, never forsake!

I shared these words. Fear was removed. God continued to protect, and the words gave a new determination.

I find prayer is a two-way communication. Sometimes I find myself praying, "God, I cannot pray. Give me the words I need." God provides and keeps the communication open. Often, God gives us *songs*. Many times the words to the songs are like preludes or even overtures to the answers to the prayers we have prayed.

I remember hearing a very special lady include in every prayer I heard her pray, "Our heavenly Father, we thank you for keeping us from seen and unseen dangers" At the time, I remembered the words more in anticipation of what was coming next in the prayers, for I had nearly committed the repeated phrases to memory, subconsciously. Now, those words find their way into many of my prayer thoughts, or sentence thanks, and they are very real. When I sing, "Through many dangers, toils, and snares, I have already come," my subconscious is saying, "Thank you for keeping me from seen and unseen dangers." The song is real.

My mother suffered a massive coronary and lay in a coma for nearly a month, with each day bringing a new breakdown to a primary body function. My desire and prayers for her recovery in the light of such opposite bodily response confused me. In the midst of all my questions, the Lord directed me to a song which I had heard before, but never sung nor consciously remembered:

> He giveth more grace when the burdens grow greater,
> He sendeth more strength when the labors increase,
> To added affliction He addeth His mercy,
> To multiplied trials, His multiplied peace.
> His love has no limit, His grace has no measure,

> His power has no boundary known unto man;
> For out of His infinite riches in Jesus,
> He giveth, and giveth, and giveth again!
>
> Amie Johnson Flint from *Hymns for the Family of God,* no. 112. "He Giveth More Grace"

Prayer that surfaced in the form of questions was being answered within these lyrics. I was reassured that my earthly loss would be my mother's heavenly gain and my ultimate hope. The greater assurance was that I was not alone: "He promised never to leave me, never to leave me alone."

Even more recently I watched my sister, forty-nine years old, carry the dreaded cross of cancer in such a glorious witnessing that there is no doubt in my mind but that her cross is now her crown. She was never a singer, but she said to me and to a close friend on the day before the light of recognition was to leave her eyes, "Let's sing!" I said, "What shall we sing?" I made several suggestions, all of which were rejected. Then remembering that her prayer that day had been, "Lord, have mercy," followed by a praise offering of "Thank you, Lord," I began to sing, "Oh, Lord, have mercy." She said, "Yes, that's it! The three of us joined in this prayer song, singing it at least three times. The next day, a blank look replaced that of recognition, more systems broke down, and life was something to endure until the soul could break loose from its prison to that greater life. But we had prayed together a prayer song, and when she could not visibly nor audibly pray, the request of the prayer showed forth its answer through the loving care of the people in the hospice, the shared love of family, and the memory of her prayers of thanksgiving in the midst of her suffering.

During my sister's illness, I received a letter from an older friend which it seems appropriate to share in this writing about prayers in song:

Dear Charlotte,

    I was in the congregation last Sunday when the Minister spoke of your sister's illness. My only thought at the time was compassion for a Christian sister, her trials and tribulations in the past few years. Yet, I knew God would sustain you and keep you in His care, as He has done in the past.

    I will pass on to you these hymns which I would always sing when my burdens seemed too heavy:

> Pass Me Not, O, Gentle Savior
> He Knows Just How Much We Can Bear
> Take Your Burden to the Lord, and Leave It There.

I'm sure He heard me, as my spirit would always be renewed. Charlotte, take care, and may God bless and keep you.

Mrs. Gamby

I thank God for the gift of song and for the healing ministry it gives to each of us.

Acknowledgements

Selections from *Strength to Love* reprinted by permission of Joan Daves. Copyright © 1963 by Martin Luther King, Jr.

Selections from *Liberation and Unity: A Lenten Booklet* used by permission of the Consultation on Church Union.

Selections from *Free to Choose* by Mary Adebonojo are copyright © 1980 by the Executive Council of the Episcopal Church, Commission on Black Ministry. Reprinted with permission of Judson Press.

Selected lines from "I Sing Your Praises All Day Long" in *Young African at Prayer* edited by Fritz Pawelzik, Friendship Press, New York. Copyright 1967, published in German (under the title "Ich Singe Dein Lob Den Tag") by Aussaat Verlag, Wuppertal. W. Germany.

"Christmas Prayer" by James A. Forbes, Jr. in *Outstanding Black Sermons Volume 3*, copyright 1982, Judson Press. Used by permission of Judson Press.

Prayer "I am happy" by a young African from *Sing and Pray and Shout Hurray!* compiled by Roger Ortmayer. Copyright Friendship Press, New York, 1974. Used by permission.

Prayers by J. Solomon Benn, III in *Preaching from the Bible* published by Baker Book House, 1981. Used by permission.

Verse 3 of "Lift Every Voice and Sing" (James Weldon Johnson, J. Rosamond Johnson) © Copyright: Edward B. Marks Music Company. Used by permission.

"Lead Me to Calvary" by Jennie Evelyn Hussey © 1921. Renewal 1949 by Hope Publishing Co., Carol Stream, IL. All rights reserved. Used by permission.

Selected prayers from *Stars At Your Fingertips* by Martin Luther Harvey used by permission of Clarie Collins Harvey.

"Lord, Help Me to Hold Out" by James Cleveland reprinted by permission of Dr. J. Jefferson Cleveland.

Selected prayers from *The Growing Edge* by Howard Thurman are © 1956 Howard Thurman. Published by Friends United Press. Used by permission.

"For My People" by Margaret Walker Alexander is used by permission of the author.

"A Liturgy for Celebrating the Eucharist" published by The Absalom Jones Association of the Episcopal Church at Howard University. Used by permission of Father Porter, Episcopal Chaplin, Rankin Chapel, Howard University.

Prayers by Bolga Ige in *Student at Prayer* copyright © 1960 by The Upper Room. Used by permission.

Prayers by W. Maurice King in *Soul and Soil: Thoughts by and about George Washington Carver.* Copyright © 1971 by The Upper Room. Used by permission.

Selections from *The Life Experience and Gospel Labors of the Rt. Rev. Richard Allen* published by Abingdon Press, © 1960. Bicentennial Edition 1983.

Author Index

Adams, John Hurst 72
Adebonojo, Mary 30, 52
Akers, Doris 101
Allen, Charles 105
Allen, Joseph Lincoln 71
Allen, Richard 74-80
Anderson, Charles 84
Anonymous 70
Baldwin, James 92-94
Benn, Solomon J. 87
Bethea, Joseph B. 73
Bollinger, H. D. 24
Brooks, Glenn A. 19, 40
Caldwell, Gilbert H. 73
Campbell, Rosalie M. 23, 36, 47, 48
Carroll, Edward G. 17
Carroll, Elizabeth Juanita 72
Carver, George Washington 62
Cleveland, James 103
Cone, James H. 14
Crosby, Fannie J. 97, 98
Cunningham, R. W. 55, 56, 57
Dixon, Thelma S. 16, 61, 62
Dodson, Owen 90
Dubois, W. E. B. 84
Ducree, Edward 35
Dunbar, Paul Laurence 53, 85, 86
Edmonds, Claude 26
English, Ronald 57-58
Fabio, Sara Webster 89
Flint, Amie Johnson 108
Forbes, James A. Jr. 41, 55
Hart, Betty 48
Hart, Erica 68
Harvey, M. L. 23, 27, 28, 29, 31, 35, 37, 42, 46, 52, 57
Hawkins, Walter 97
Hawks, Annie S. 105

Higgins, Elmira 44, 69
Henderson, Cornelius L. 73
Horton, Frank L. 43
Howard, Cecil W. 71
Hussey, Jennie Evelyn 100
Johnson, James Weldon 99
Johnson, Rosamond J. 99
Kincaid, LaVon 34
King, Maurice W. 36, 54, 66
Killens, John O. 91-92
Lawson, James 37, 46, 49
LeRoi, Jones 96
Mackay, William P. 104
McClain, William B. 20, 33, 95
Miller, Levi 32, 49, 63
Moore, Josephine M. 70
Moore, Theodore A. 72
Ortmayer, Roger 71
Powell, John W. Jr. 74
Raybold, George 38
Reed, Albert L. 22
Reed, Clarence 84
Rice, Angie 68
Roberts, J. DeOtis 20
Russell, Valerie E. 71
Stovall, Leonard Charles 32, 33
Thurman, Howard 33, 36, 37, 80-81
Tindley, Charles Albert 45, 104
Turner, Eugene G. 72
Walker, Margaret 88
Walker, Wyatt Tee 15
Wesley, Charles 98
Williams, Roscoe Conklin 34
Williams, Willard A. 13, 21, 35
Woodson, M. L. 21, 47

Richard Bowyer is Campus Minister of The Wesley Foundation at Fairmont State College. Reverend Bowyer received the Master of Divinity and Master of Theology degrees from Duke University. He serves as editor of the journal, *Toward Wholeness*.

Betty Hart is Instructor of English at Fairmont State College, Fairmont, West Virginia. She received the Master of Arts degree from West Virginia University in Morgantown, West Virginia and is studying for her doctorate.

Charlotte Meade teaches eighth grade Language Arts in Marion County, West Virginia. She received the Master of Education degree from the University of Toledo in Ohio. Ms. Meade also serves as Choir Director of Trinity United Methodist Church.